THE IMPACT
OF AUSTERITY MEASURES
ON PEOPLE AND LOCAL GOVERNMENT

THE IMPACT
OF AUSTERITY MEASURES
ON PEOPLE AND LOCAL GOVERNMENT

Sebwa Domingos

authorHOUSE®

AuthorHouse™ UK
1663 Liberty Drive
Bloomington, IN 47403 USA
www.authorhouse.co.uk
Phone: 0800.197.4150

Published by AuthorHouse 10/28/2014

ISBN: 978-1-4969-9478-3 (sc)
ISBN: 978-1-4969-9479-0 (hc)
ISBN: 978-1-4969-9480-6 (e)

To the memory of my beloved mother,
Cristina de Lima Nunes Soeiro Domingos (1948–2011).

Acknowledgements

The writing of this book has been a long-term project, during which I have incurred many debts. While most of the process of producing this type of work demanded numerous hours of lonely creativity and intellectual rigour, many people have provided me incalculable aid in my efforts to bring this book into existence during the past five years.

First and foremost, I would like to thank my father for being such a source of inspiration and for providing me with the environment that enabled me to become the man I am now. Words cannot describe what he means to me and how grateful and proud I am to be his son.

Secondly, I am grateful to academic staff In department of Law, Governance and International Relations (LGIR) at London metropolitan university. Special thanks to Pat Gray, for pedagogical suggestions and contributions for chapter order of the manuscript; Dr Mike Mills, for willingness and incessant support; Dr Diana Stirbu for providing academic down to earth wit and comment on my work.

Sebwa Domingos

I also gratefully acknowledge the support and help that my partner and my family (brothers, sisters, and cousins) have provided throughout my ups and down during this project.

Last but not least, I thank my friends and former colleagues who helped sustain me with their philosophical discussions and who gave me some practical and technical assistance and support in regard to some computer issues. Again, errors and omissions are my sole responsibility.

Despite all my efforts, in some instances I have been unable to trace the owners of copyrights, and I would greatly appreciate any information that would enable me to do so.

Contents

Illustrations

Figures

1. Local-government (LG) pyramid
2. Connection between people, local government, and central government

Tables

1. One-tier (unitary) council responsibilities

2. Two-tier council responsibilities
3. Council-tax property band valuation
4. Number of working-age people claiming key benefits
5. Benefit expenditure per year – London Borough of Hackney
6. Benefit expenditure per year – Royal Borough of Kensington and Chelsea (K&C)
7. Number of households renting in social housing – Hackney and K&C

Abbreviations

BBC – British Broadcasting Corporation
BME – Black and Minority Ethnic
BoE – Bank of England
BRICS – Brazil, Russia, India, China, South Africa
CRE – Commission for Racial Equality
DCLG – Department for Communities and Local Government
DWP – Department for Work and Pensions
EC – European Commission
ECB – European Central Bank
EGO – Extra-Governmental Organization
EHRC – Equal and Human Rights Commission
EMA – Employment Maintenance Allowance
ESA – Employment Support Allowance
EU – European Union
FSA – Food Standards Agency
GDP – Gross Domestic Product
GLA – Greater London Authority
GLC – Greater London Corporation
IFS – Institute for Fiscal Studies
IMF – International Monetary Fund

IT – Information Technology
JSA – Jobseeker's Allowance
K&C – (Royal Borough of) Kensington and Chelsea
LAs – Local Authorities
LCs – Local Councils
LG – Local Government
LGA – Local Government Authority
MNCs – Multinational Corporations
NICs – National Insurance Contributions
NIESR – National Institute for Economic and Social Research
NNDR – National Non-Domestic Rate
OBR – Office for Budget Responsibility
ONS – Office for National Statistics
Quangos – Quasi-Autonomous Non-Governmental Organizations
RDAs – Regional Development Agencies
RSG – Revenue Support Grant
S&P – Standard & Poor
SAPs – Structural Adjustment Programmes
SSA – Standard Spending Assessment
TNC – Transnational Corporation
UK – United Kingdom
UN – United Nations
US(A) – United States (of America)
VOA – Valuation Office Agency
WB – World Bank

Introduction

Austerity measures have been given an increased public profile within the UK policy agenda in the past few years. Since late 2010, austerity has become a theme of considerable contemporary public interest and debate. Austerity measures were employed during economic recession in order to deal with huge government sovereign debts and/ or to counterbalance massive structural government budget deficits. Similar to her European counterparts, the British government embarked on austerity measures in order to reduce the huge national deficit and debt, an idea that is seen as dangerous in some quarters.

So far, despite all good efforts to bring public cuts to manageable levels, these austerity measures have failed to produce satisfactory results. The UK national debt net stands at £1.3 trillion, equivalent to 77.3 per cent of the gross domestic product (GDP). Even though the latest economic statistics have shown a robust improvement in the overall state of the UK economy – with growth at around 3.5 per cent, the highest since the pre-recession period – the government is trying to portray that people of all walks of life will be better off with austerity in place, irrespective of their social status, age, race, gender, and so on.

Quite simply, the economic growth figure is masking the truth. There is a great deal of evidence showing that austerity measures are having a disproportional effect on some people and some localities. Indeed, individual people across Britain are worse off than they were before austerity measures were put in place. They are not receiving a fair share of the rewards of the economic growth. The cost of living, inflation, and stagnant incomes have worsened the financial conditions of a great number of people across the UK. As a result, the number of people relying on food banks and facing hardship has increased in the last three years. In addition, the gap between the haves and have-nots has widened, with the very rich seeing their incomes rise, while the bulk of the population has not seen any wage increase in real terms, which results in squeezed standards of living. What is more, such groups as women, young people, black and minority ethnic (BME), people with disabilities, and low-income people are the ones hit hardest by the cuts in public spending. The impact of austerity measures will be felt even more acutely in years to come, particularly by young people, who will face decades of stagnation due to high levels of unemployment in that group. On top of the stagnation is the reform of welfare benefits, which now impose tougher sanctions and conditions for receiving social security benefits.

This book seeks to analyse the effect of austerity measures on people and local government (LG) in the United Kingdom. The pace in which draconian cuts have been wielded by coalition-led Conservatives has allowed LG a little room to manoeuvre and devise good strategies to deal with huge loss of revenue in local budgets. In order to be analytically useful, we must be clear about what austerity measures are and how they impact people and localities in the UK. Unfortunately, this is by no means self-evident, in the sense that the notion of austerity measures remains a contested terrain. However, the impact of austerity measures on people and places in the UK is well documented.

The people subject to our studies are those in low-paying jobs and those who rely on the state to provide services, such as BME, women, young people, lone parents, people with disabilities, and elderly people. Historically, austerity measures have encompassed welfare cuts rather than tax increases, and such cuts in turn affect those who are more likely to be dependent on state provisions. That said, we must start from the simple premise that, historically, BME, women, young people, and people with disabilities have been more likely to be in lower-paying jobs. Therefore, cuts in public spending will have a significant and disproportional effect on the people cited above and the places where they live.

Austerity measures have produced very patchy results; in many cases, countries that embarked on cutting public spending have seen their economies deteriorate. Until recently, austerity measures have been used and experimented with around the world. However, welfare reform failed to kick-start economic development. Reports published by the World Bank (WB), the International Monetary Fund (IMF), the United Nations (UN), and numerous academic sources appear to back this up. For example, several countries throughout Latin America, Asia, and Africa embarked on austerity measures – also known as structural adjustment programmes (SAPs) – with catastrophic results. However, two countries – Canada and Sweden – stand out from the rest and are held up as models of successfully reduced public deficits by means of austerity measures. That said, the extent to which austerity measures impact people will vary from place to place. Our argument is that austerity is a dangerous idea, and governments should only use it to please international creditors and retain the credibility of market investors.

Organization of the book

Austerity measures are on the agendas of most Western European countries. With public debt crippling nations and spiralling out control, the implementation of austerity measures is undoubtedly one the most debated issues in contemporary politics.

The central objective of the book is to consider the impact of austerity measures upon people and LG by exploring the different aspects and dimensions in which cuts to public service affect people in different areas. In other words, it is a book of comparative analysis. The traditional emphasis of comparative studies analysis is to compare and contrast arguments of various government policies by drawing on specialist knowledge so as to produce new and more general observations. To answer the question, we must first start from the assumption that local authorities (LAs) have similarities and dissimilarities; they have a differing households, structural compositions, and political allegiances that are important for both political and economic outcomes.

The key themes within each chapter of this book are informed and driven by the literature, each covering a distinctive and important narrative aspect of the impact of austerity measures on people and places in the UK.

Chapter 1 deals with the conceptual view of austerity measures and then discusses the merits and demerits of implementing austerity measures. Indeed, it sets out some philosophical arguments to explain which group of people will be more likely to be disproportional affected by austerity measures, and why. People on social benefits and people in lower-paying jobs are generally the most likely to be affected by cuts in public spending.

In chapter 2, we give an account for the rationale underpinning coalition government's decision to cut public services. It is our intention to explain the role of liberal theory in economics and the allocation of good and services. The argument here is that the notion of austerity measures is underpinned by ideological views rather than empirical scientific evidence. Austerity measures are used as a pretext to reduce greatly the government's huge sovereign debt; but in reality, these measures aim to prove that government is serious about balancing budgets, winning back investors' confidence, and retaining it. It is indeed a neo-liberal view that coalition government's ideas derive from, but it is based on Swedish and Canadian successes, from which such governments have gained comfort. (You will recall that Sweden and Canada have successfully reduced public debt by embarking on austerity measures.)

Chapter 3 deals with local government in the UK. The aim is to provide a concise and a comprehensive introduction of the history of local government in the UK by tracing how it evolved over the years. The intention is also to give readers a clear understanding of the structures and processes of local government in the UK. This chapter sets the tone for the rest of book by highlighting two distinct features that make it increasingly difficult for LG to implement policies aimed towards local citizens. Firstly, the UK does not have a written constitution, and Parliament is sovereign. Secondly, the raising of revenue of local government depends on compliance with strict central-government rules and regulations.

Chapter 4 examines the extent to which government welfare reform affects localities and the ways in which some domestic policies are influenced by factors beyond central-government control. Two reasons are given here. One is the shift in the welfare system, with tougher conditions and sanctions attached to getting social security benefits. Another is the process of globalization, which has brought new challenges to nation states that undermine their capacity to make their own decisions. New networks and agencies have become major players in the process of decision-making, and this limits the powers of nation states. Such agencies include the IMF, WB, and UN, as previously mentioned, as well as multinational corporations (MNCs), the European Union (EU), and so on. Globalization and the work of these organizations have also brought people together; thus, what happens in one place affects people in other nations. Some others factors, such as changes in demographics in the UK population, are also linked to globalization. (For example, migration was made possible by access to cheaper air travel, advances in medicine, and so on.)

Chapter 5 provides an assessment for exploring whether austerity measures are working – or not. Indeed, it sheds a light measuring whether austerity approaches reduce or increase the well-being of the neediest in the society.

Chapter 6 considers the impact of austerity measures in two LAs in the UK. These two English LAs located in London: the Royal Borough of Kensington and Chelsea (K&C) and the London Borough of Hackney. The starting point here is that the impact of cutbacks will be felt differently by people depending on where they live. Here, our analysis is focused on assessing the impact of austerity measures on the LAs cited above and the effects on local residents.

The extent to which austerity measures impact people at the local level is determined by numerous factors, such as demographic composition of households, local traditions, political pressures, party influences and disciplines, bureaucratic professionalism, level of economic development, council tax base, and so on. Having said that, we believe that these attributes ought to be taken into account when measuring the impact of austerity on people and LAs. So political imperatives along government economic policies rather than social needs may play a role in deciding which boroughs are more affected.

The conclusion summarizes the key issues and debates on which both theories and practice rely on, and concludes that at present there is a great deal of evidence to argue that the effects of austerity measures on people and on local government is at best overlooked.

Methodology of the book

This book explores the impact of austerity measures upon people, especially in two LAs (K&C and Hackney). It considers a number of questions, most importantly:

- Are austerity measures desirable and/or feasible?
- To what extent does change in eligibility for social benefits impact people, and why?

It is important to bear in mind that the topic is highly complex. Therefore, this book uses mixed methodology; that is, we use a combination of techniques ranging from literature review (historical, political, and global perspective) to primary resources. In the first instance, it may rely more on the historical and political/global approaches than the primary resources. Nonetheless, this book does use primary resources and theoretical perspectives interchangeably to argue our case. Primary resources will be used in order to assess the recent trends on the impact of austerity measures, especially the extent to which that impact affects poor people. The basis of methodology informing it will be looking at the most up-to-date data in order to find whether there is a correlation between the reduction in public expenditures of LAs and the reform of welfare (changes in policies with regard to eligibility for social benefits), since austerity measures were imposed by coalition government in 2010. Sufficiently similar cases cannot be found. Most of this study deals with easily quantifiable data analysis, nevertheless an important area of public spending and budgetary analysis. The emphasis on this approach is to respond to what is believed to be the great political and moral imperatives linked to it.

As previously mentioned, the two LAs we will be looking at are English LAs with predominantly urban populations. Hackney and K&C are inner London LAs; one is Labour Party majority controlled local authority (LA), and the other is a Conservative Party majority controlled LA. The indicators will be in two forms: Firstly, we will look at the impact of reduction in the LA public spending power. Secondly, we will look at how government policy changes are having detrimental effects on the provision of social services to people in the two LAs (Hackney and K&C).

Some of these indicators include:

- The impact of staff reduction on service delivery
- Reduction in or withdrawal of provision of certain services
- Increase in number of jobseeker's allowance (JSA) applications
- Increase in number of people claiming out-of-work benefits
- Increase in number of people claiming housing benefits

I have chosen to take this approach because I wish to emphasize one aspect of topic. However, adopting a singular approach may have oversimplified the issue as whole. Even the best-laid plans can sometimes produces unexpected results. Like any other social research approach, data monitoring trends does have its flaws. Therefore, the problem of using this method as main indicator to assess the extent to which austerity measures impact people in the two LAs is that it will ignore greatly other possible and equally relevant changes.

Furthermore, factors which would represent national diversity, such as language and class, probably would be least relevant in terms of policy, whereas those factors which are most likely to influence policy (e.g. political ideology or level of economic development) present more theoretical and statistical problems to manage.

Research involves working with people and gathering information about people's lives. Therefore, safeguarding the confidentiality of respondents is paramount. Researchers must be aware of sensitivity and safety issues that may arise when collecting this type of data. There are is a set of rules that researchers must comply with, such as seeking consent prior to the study and maintaining the anonymity of the participants.

All cases studies here reflect the impact of austerity measures on gender, location, ethnicity, and voting (political affiliation), but they exhibit chronic disagreements. It is not merely a matter of different methods producing results. The economy analysis appears to agree about the extent and basis of local variation, while the survey-based work differs completely regarding gender, class, location, and ethnicity. The fact that we have to collect statistical data from different sources with different figures, because there no analogous websites on spending for LAs, makes it difficult to totally assess like-to-like cases. However, data available from different Internet sources on LAs' current spending proved very helpful, providing valuable data on current and past years, which allowed us to make comparisons rather than future predictions. Hence, the value of conclusions will be limited by the quality of the data used.

Having discussed the book's organization and methodology, let's move on to chapter 1, where we will examine who faces the cuts generated by the implementation of austerity measures.

CHAPTER 1

Austerity measures: who face the cuts?

For the purpose of our discussion in this book, it is pertinent to give conceptual explanations as to why austerity measures are taken and what their implementation entails. At the most general level, austerity measures have come to be associated with any economic reform programme taking place. So to dissipate that, we must first define what we mean by austerity measures. The term *austerity measures* is by no means easily quantified; however, this book refer to austerity measures in economic terms, as a policy of deficit reduction that is achieved by lowering spending via reducing the amount of benefits and public services (*Financial Times* 2010). Governments often employ austerity measures in order to reduce deficit spending; such measures are sometimes coupled with increases in taxes in order to demonstrate long-term fiscal solvency to international creditors (Traynor and Allen 2010). Austerity measures are evolving and contested, and they differ in effects between different levels of governments and sectors. As a rule, austerity measures are taken when a government fears that it will not be able to honour its debt obligations (IMF 2010).

Proponents of austerity claim that a major reduction in government spending can change future expectations about government spending, encouraging private consumption and resulting in overall economic expansion (Alesina and Ardagna 2002). On the other hand, critics argue that in periods of recession and high unemployment, austerity policies are counterproductive because reduced government spending can increase unemployment, which increases safety-net spending while reducing tax revenue. That is to say, reduction in government spending will have repercussions on GDP, as the debt of GDP ratio is measured by creditors, and so the nation's standing with rating agencies will not improve (Westbury and Robert 2010).

Bach and Stroleny (2013) argue that government deficit-reduction programmes are in response to pressure put on countries by market bond. Governments operate in a volatile economic and political environment; therefore, market forces and other key actors exert pressure in the way governments respond to economic and social issues (Bach and Stroleny 2013). Thus, it could be concluded that adoption of austerity measure is primarily motivated to reassure financial markets.

Again, since austerity measures entail a reduction in the amount of benefits and public services, implementation of such measures will have numerous implications for people in the UK. The impact of austerity on people and localities can either be negative or positive. Throughout this book, we will highlight the impact that reduction in public spending can have upon some groups of people and some localities in the UK.

The UK has changed considerably in recent years, ever since some types of discrimination were outlawed. Since the 1970s, the population of Great Britain has grown form less than 55 million to over 64.1 million (ONS 2014). This includes 1 million more men and 0.6 million more women aged 65 or over. There were 9.4 million adults over 65 in 2005, representing 16 per cent of the population. Out of 24 million households, there were 7 million families with dependent children. There were also 10 million people with disabilities and over

4.5 million ethnic minority communities, an increase of 50 per cent between the 1991 census and the 2001 census (ONS 2011).

Britain is in many ways a fairer and more egalitarian society than at any time in living memory, and many of us enjoy a lifestyle far richer and less restricted than ever before. Nevertheless, even though some of the issues facing disadvantaged people have been successfully reduced, it seems that there are still deep-seated disadvantages for some groups (Pearce and Paxton 2005). For example, women still face the gender pay gap, and representation is virtually non-existent. The lack of women and BME in top jobs and in Parliament is glaring (Barbara 2009).

Broadly speaking, coalition government cuts to public services will have a disproportional effect on people. Who are the ones who will be most affected? For our purposes in this book, we will refer to people who rely on government services and benefits as a main source of income, and also to those who are employed in lower-paying jobs and occupations in either the public or private sector, such as women, BME, people with disabilities, elderly people, young people, refugees, and asylum seekers (Platt 2005; Mason 2003). Low pay means that these individuals don't earn enough money to be able to afford to heat their homes or provide the bare essentials for themselves and their dependents. There are several reasons that can explain this. Historically, BME, women, and people with disabilities have found it easier to gain employment in the public sector (www.hmso.gov.uk). Approximately 40 per cent of BME workers are employed in public service, compared to 25 per cent of white counterparts. In addition, women, BME, and people with disabilities tend to have lower-paying jobs and occupations (Platt 2005; Pearce and Paxton 2005; Hills et al. 2007). They also tend to live in more-deprived areas. Finally, they are more likely to abstain from voting in general elections (IFS 2013). Conventional views stress that the deepest and most sustained cuts were targeted on areas with a high index of deprivation (both rural and urban areas), as well as in areas with a higher rate of abstaining during the political process (Dorling and Thomas 2011).

Again, among the councils that suffered the highest cuts in public expenditure were those boroughs ranked in the top of the most deprived LAs in England during the last five years, including Doncaster, Liverpool, Manchester, and the London Borough of Hackney (*The Guardian* 2013; IFS 2013). Therefore, as jobs cuts and pay freezes take effect, it's not hard to see who will bear the brunt of the pain. According to the Equal and Human Rights Commission (EHRC), research has found that BME groups earn less than whites. In particular, black male graduates earn 24 per cent less than white British male graduates. Inequality is also evident in regard to the gender pay gap. It is clear that at present the most immediate threat to the majority of women, BME, and people with disabilities is government spending cuts to social services. Researchers say that Caribbean blacks earned more per hour than whites before the recession; however, that statistic has reversed ever since the Conservatives took over (*The Guardian* 2013). As austerity measures start to bite the public, the impact will be felt, and with particular severity by the groups mentioned above. Again, because the public sector is a source of stability and employment for them.

What is more, the research consistently highlights that women and BME are bearing the brunt of the cuts to public spending, with record numbers of women out of work, and the majority of welfare cuts coming from women's pockets; essential services are under threat, and women are expected to plug the gaps. The repercussions will be numerous. As a result, we face a future of fewer BME working, more women in poverty, the gap between white and BME widening in terms of income and earning potential, BME financial autonomy weakened, and basic rights to safety under threat.

While the government has done what it can do to portray cuts to spending as reaching into all pockets, the reality is that some people in the UK are more negatively affected than others, and women are one the groups affected badly. Women are overrepresented in the public sector, where they make up of 65 per cent of workforce. Consequently, women will be disproportionately affected by the redundancies and pay freezes which affect and reduce greatly their income. Changes in the way social benefits are made will likely bring additional pressure to bear on women because various benefits will either be cut or capped, some services will be withdrawn, and the high cost of day centres and lack of availability of nursery places will persist.

Rather than making the UK continue to move forward on the path to equality, austerity measures have now caused that forward motion to go into reverse. That is the problem, and women are one group of people to be hit hardest. The reason for this, as mentioned previously, is that, historically, women were excluded from full citizenship, which included political rights (i.e. the right to vote). Consequently, women in present-day Britain earn, on average, less than men and are far less equally represented in positions of high office and top jobs (White 2007). Women were not granted full citizenship till the 1960s; so, until very recently, exclusion of women from political rights was the norm. Poverty, nationally and globally, disproportionately affects women; of the 1.2 billion people in the world living on less than $1.00 per day, 70 per cent are women. Of 0.9 billion people in the world who are illiterate, twice as many are women (Barbara 2009). What's more, white woman, and BME women and men, are likely to be concentrated in lower-paying jobs. In addition, any government policy to reduce public expenditure and welfare reform leading to closure of day centres and elderly day care, which has a disproportional effect on women as the major caregivers in the society (White 2009). In light of all this, we can see how adversely and disproportionately these cuts impact women.

Moreover, Darlington (2012) suggests that had the cuts focused more on tax rise, as opposed to spending cuts, the burden would have been more justly distributed. The reason why it would make more sense is that tax rise affects those at top of the pile more severely than those at the bottom, so low-paid people would have been better protected from most of the cuts in spending for social services.

Britain's deficit is the legacy of a spending boom that delivered schools, hospitals, and roads before ending in 2008, when the recession began because of the collapse of the banking system (Haseler 2010). The deficit stands at more than 11 per cent of GDP. Explanations as to why the people mentioned above are most likely to be affected by austerity measures vary, and we will now explore these variations in greater detail now.

It is the view of Held et al. (2007) that poor people – women, BME, people with disabilities, young people, and elderly people – suffer from a variety of deficiencies, ranging from a lack of education, to an inability to properly participate in decision-making, to an insufficiency of many other life essentials. The result is that they lack political clout and are more likely to abstain from voting (Hills et al. 2005; Pearce and Paxton 2005). On the other end of the spectrum, that of the very rich, cuts in public spending would attract less opposition than raising taxes (Dorling and Thomas 2011). Regardless of which reason we consider, or a combination thereof, the end result is that the disadvantaged continue to suffer.

In the foregoing discussion, we have emphasized the advantages and disadvantages of austerity measures. In the next chapter, we shall consider major criticisms that have been levelled against the cutting of public spending.

CHAPTER 2

A rationale for austerity: critique and analysis

As we have seen, government austerity measures hit hardest the people in society who are the most vulnerable. While some attention has been rightly devoted to the impact of austerity measures on poor people and their neighbourhoods, very little has been written to explain how and where these policies come from. This chapter seeks to provide a framework which will assist us in understanding the rationale that motivates government intervention in economic, political, and social affairs. Our main concern is not to give an account of the rationale for all government actions, but it is our intention to explain the role that neo-liberal theory plays in economic affairs and in the provision of public services.

British economic policies and British business have long been dominated by perspectives originating in banking and trade rather than industry. This has given both an international orientation, which liberal political economy, with its emphasis on markets, perfectly expresses (Gamble 1994). The size and importance of the financial sector was enhanced because the British government depended on it to fund the national debt and control the money supply (Gamble

1994). The most important factor has been the external dependence of the British economy on the world economy, which the policy of free trade helped create in the first place. Gamble argues that this basic reality of British position has enormously reinforced the tendency to view Britain's problems from the standpoint of the world market. As a result, national policy has been conceived to adjust the national economy to world economic conditions (Gamble 1994).

Academic opinions over explanations of austerity measures in the economic and political literature vary. Nonetheless, the orthodox view appears to be that its root can be associated with liberal views that emphasize the minimal role of government in the economy. The UK government's economic policies are informed by liberal economic views that hold the idea of free trade with deregulation of markets and laissez-faire, which means that a balance of the books should be done to keep economic obligations with creditors whilst maintaining the conditions for free and expanding markets. Therefore, cutting public spending is seen as desirable for achieving economic and political credibility, primarily in order to convince the creditors (markets, investors) that the UK government can fulfil her financial obligations. Secondly, it is desirable for convincing the electorate that the Conservative Party has a better economic strategy for getting the UK economy out of recession and reducing the deficit altogether. Nonetheless, Dan (1997) claims that the economic mess is primarily a consequence of the size of the public services (i.e. social services). This claim reflects the way in which the Conservative Party views public services. For them, public services are seen as ineffective, inefficient, and wasteful of government resources.

In the UK, the main driver has been high internal pressure within the coalition government committed to austerity. Bach and Stroleny (2013) identify two distinctive factors for the adoption of austerity measures in the UK: internal and external. There are high and low pressures domestically, and to certain extent, external pressures have played a part as well. There has been a strong commitment towards fiscal consolidation by the Conservative-led coalition in office in the UK since 2010. The immediate trigger's main justification for phased reduction in public expenditure has been the coalition's commitment to a fiscal mandate aiming to achieve expenditure balance by 2015–16. The underlying economic assumptions and political ideology of the coalition government constitute important drivers towards austerity. The starting point is criticism of the previous Labour government's expansion of big government, as reflected in the growth of the public-sector workforce and pay bill. The coalition government agreement stated that deficit reduction and economic recovery were the most urgent issues facing Britain (Cabinet office 2010). The government persists in this view today, maintaining that continuing to ensure economic recovery is of paramount importance.

Furthermore, the rationale underpinning the UK government is that austerity measures worked before. The introduction of cuts in public spending by the government in Canada and Sweden during the economic recession in the 1990s helped to tackle successfully the deficits of those two countries. Between 1993 and 2000, they slashed spending share of GDP by 12 per cent, and vigorous economic growth driven by a rejuvenated private sector followed. Therefore, the coalition government in the UK, seeing the relative success of Canada and Sweden, as appealing, decided that theirs was a good example to follow. Critics of Canada's model point out that it was rolled out at a time of major growth in the United States, which generated demands for Canadian goods. By contrast, at present a country cannot rely as much as before on external demand to help cushion the impact of consolidation on growth, because Britain's biggest market, the eurozone, and many of the advanced economies are growing slowly or not at all. In addition to this, Canada also had room to cut interest rates, while the British monetary system cannot be loosened up any further.

Another interesting point is that the Conservatives perceive public services as wasteful of government resources and inferior when compared to services provided by the private sector. The belief is that public services are bureaucratic, monopolistic, and excessively administered – all of which resulted in a waste of resources and an indifference to customer needs and preferences. For Conservatives, adopting private-sector techniques in public services would greatly improve efficiency and would also compel the public services to be more responsive to customers. It is the view of Dan (1997) that public service, as an entity, is spiralling out control, as a result of pressure on the system, much of which stems from the from the size of welfare. It also argued that current structure of welfare state and discourage saving and effort. The Conservative Party and their Liberal Democrat Party partners in government share this view. However, it is not the current structure of the welfare state that discourages saving and efforts to save; rather, it is the current monetary policy, with lower interest (0.5per cent), which discourages saving.

It is for ideological and doctrinaire reasons that the Conservative Party decided to embark on austerity measures in the first place. Conservatives are hostile to public services, and their perspective is informed by neo-liberal traditions which posit that markets and private property dictate who gets what in a given society (Byrne 1997).

Thus far, the bulk of savage cuts have been on welfare benefits and public services, which hit the poor hardest, as opposed to raising taxes, which would affect the wealthy. This reveals much about the coalition government's economic policies, as influenced by neo-liberal ideas that see inequality as the result of market imperfections (Held et al. 2007; Byrne 1997). This may also be significant in explaining why there were very few substantially tax rises so far. A reason for this might lie in the pattern of distribution of resources, which tend to favour the preference of the wealthy people in the society who have the adequate means to articulate and influence political decisions (Held et al. 2007).

Another reason can be that cuts in public and welfare services are less likely to attract less opposition, as compared with raising taxes. Cutting public services and welfare benefits means hitting hardest the pockets of poor people, as we have already concluded, and because they lack the connections to exert pressure and to lobby government, their upset causes little trouble for politicians. In other words, poor people lack the adequate connections and the means to articulate and influence the political process, and even to participate in it; whereas those at the top of the societal ladder possess both the connections and the means, and they participate in the political process quite vigorously.

Again, Dorling and Thomas (2011) point to the fact that the vast bulk of cuts were concentrated in areas with high levels of vote abstentions, or where constituents voted against the two parties that formed the coalition government in the general election. Given this evidence, we can see that the personality and power of the past and present British Conservative prime ministers play a part as well. These individuals have a long-standing and deep-seated dislike of local government and public services, which has been exploited as way to fulfil long-standing ambitions to take control and reward boroughs who voted for them (Dorling and Thomas 2011). This curious combination has led to economics which threaten not only to strip LAs of their financial autonomy but also to punish those who voted against them in the last general elections.

Let's now look at arguments against the idea that privately owned companies always perform better in the competitive market than publicly owned ones. The evidence is mixed, but it seems to suggest that private enterprise is generally preferred in terms of both internal efficiency and social welfare (Dan 1997). However, this does not mean that public enterprise is always the less efficient type of ownership in the competitive market. In fact, no simple generalizations about the superiority of private-sector performance can be sustained. Furthermore, according Bach and Stroleny (2013), the relative size of a nation's public services bears no relations to austerity measures. They argue that Denmark has a very sizeable public sector but low levels of debt; thus, austerity pressures have been muted. In contrast, Italy has a relatively low share of public services but a high debt burden, and still she has adopted austerity measures to reduce debts.

It is clear from a wide array of literature that shifts in the labour market, demographic changes, economic and government policies allied to the process of globalization, and electoral imperatives played a role in the reform of welfare policy (Sawyer 2005; Taylor-Gooby et al. 2001). It is indeed the application of economic principles and deregulated markets, along with demographic shifts, that led the UK economy into disarray, rather than pressure on the system caused by the huge size of public services and welfare, as Dan (1997) appears to suggest. Broadly speaking, there is public support for the view that the current deficit must be reduced. However, the problem may lie in the policies previously put in place by the Conservative Party in the early 1980s, as influenced by neo-liberal views. At that time, the cuts in public spending and taxation were made in assertion that they would roll back the boundaries of the state and return power to the people. The benefits of these policies would then emerge in economic growth which in turn would trickle down to those less fortunate (Broadshaw 1996). That was the promise. It has been nearly four decades since the Conservative Party first embarked on the privatization process, trying to roll back the state. Yet the UK government remains the most centralized government of any Western nation in the world, with too much power concentrated in the hands of central government (in Westminster, London).

Another point is that the decision to end the link between the adjustment of some benefits and earnings has ensured that the income of those attached to the labour market and those dependent on benefits have become increasingly divided (Broadshaw 1996). In fact, cutting social spending leads to one two-part result: it stops the poor and the middle class from buying anything, and it encourages the rich to hold onto their wealth. Squeezed customers won't create demand until they have the confidence that they can spend a bit more and manage their debts (Darlington 2012).

As cited above, austerity measures and policies have been tried and used before, and the results have been patchy. Even in successful cases, many poor people were no better off after the measures were in place, and many were actually poorer than they had been previously (Haynes 2005). To put this another way, even the recovery effect gains usually fall in the top 1 per cent – that is, the very rich. In fact, there is much hard evidence indicating that poverty has grown in recent years, after the welfare reforms failed to kick-start economic growth. IMF structural adjustment programmes (SAPs) throughout the developing world illustrate the negative impact of welfare reforms imposed on the poor. It is suggested that the IMF has learnt from its experiences in the late 1990s, when austerity budgetary demands backfired in Indonesia, South Korea, and Thailand, causing deep recessions in all three countries (*New York Times* 2012). This led the head of the IMF to warn the British government of the perils of embarking on austerity measures, stating that is the UK was playing with fire. Above all, as Haseler (2010) perceptively states, these cuts are a response to growing government deficits, yet the key problem is that these deficits are simply the result of much bigger catastrophe: market failure as a result of the banking-system crash (Haseler 2010). Furthermore, a recent research study carried out by Dr Prebistero (Nottingham University) and Eberhardt (IMF) looked at the impact of high debt and low growth, using data drawn from 105 and 200 years of history, but the study suggests that there is no empirical evidence between them (*Financial Times* 2014). This study further illustrates that there is no basis for the economic claim so often used by government to prove that austerity measures work.

It is clear, therefore, that thus far those who caused the deficit problems – namely, bankers and politicians – have not been penalized. Instead, it is the poor and the public services (of which local government is a part) that have been left to bear the brunt of the cuts. Dorling and Thomas (2011) have found that there is an alternative to massive cuts: reducing the wealth and income of those most closely connected to the cause of the crisis. Similarly, Wolft (2010) has put forward the idea of collecting taxes from MNCs, which use internal pricing to escape US taxation, to generate vast new government revenues in the UK. The same applies to wealthy individuals, where ending tax exemptions for the superrich and for institutions of private education would generate similar government revenues. While there is validity in this argument, a note of caution should be sounded because of the capacity of mobility among big corporations, including banks. In some cases, such measures might lead to a mass exodus in the banking sector, as banks would move elsewhere to avail themselves of a more generous tax policy (Stiglitz 2007; Sklair 2002).

It must therefore be recognized that the measures described above would be costly to the UK economy and business sector, because much of our economy is built on consumerism, debt and financial services, and safeguarding London's position as a leader in global finance, which is paramount to the Conservative-led coalition government. The taxation changes suggested above would seriously jeopardize London's position as an attractive top city in which to conduct business. Such taxation changes could also jeopardize the UK's AAA-plus economic status. Following this line of argument, in order to maintain the desired business and economic situation, reform of welfare and other social policies would come at the top of the list of government priorities. Such reforms by the government would greatly enhance UK credibility and demonstrate that the coalition government is serious about balancing the budget and fulfilling long-term economic goals – hence, reassuring markets, and winning back and retaining investors' confidence in the process.

To sum up, the feasibility or desirability of the austerity measures experiment so far has been fiercely debated. As with many debates, the conclusions reached often depend on the starting point. The starting point is that internal and external factors both play a part. That is, the success or failure will depend upon various factors internally and externally. A combination of the two factors may determine the success or failure of austerity, because customer demand internally will depend greatly on what is happening elsewhere. In particular, recovery in the eurozone, Britain's biggest economic market, is key. Demand growth in the United States is also critical, as is demand growth in new markets (such as Asia) as well as in the BRICS group of emergent economies. Competition policy is a classic example of general arrangement applying to all regions and LAs in the UK. In this context, the standard economic theory offers some clear policy, suggesting that the disadvantaged members of certain groups are a consequence of imperfections that result in market failure. However, problems have arisen because the objectives of regional and/or local policies have often been social and political rather than economic. In fact, austerity policies are driven more by ideologies to appease global markets and win back investors' confidence rather than to tackle underlying causes of deficit reduction. Even the recovery gains generally fall in the hands of those at the top of the social ladder. A reduction in public-services spending will hit hardest the individuals (and communities that lack political and financial clout – women, BME, people with disabilities, young people, and elderly people.

That said, there are some powerful changes occurring on a global scale that will have an impact on the way central- and local-government provision of services are handled. Globalization, along with rapid technological and social changes, has led to some of the powerful and irreversible forces now affecting governmental decision-making processes. (We will examine these powerful changes in greater detail in chapter 4).

Now let's move on to chapter 3, where we will discuss the functions and services of local government (LG).

Local government (LG): its responsibilities, structures, and functions

The role of local government (LG) in the past few decades has expanded at a fast pace. Moreover, the numerous functions performed by LG have expanded at the same time that pressure and supervision from the central government have increased. In recent years, we have seen a decline in the independence of cities, villages, and towns in the UK as a result of population growth in metropolitan and urban areas. This has occurred to such an extent that the financial means to cope with existing problems has greatly reduced the roles of local councils in cities, metropolitan areas, villages, and towns. The role of LG in the UK is said to be changing from that of a service provider to an enabling role.

In order to understand the significance of this, we must first examine the history of local government in the UK. LG traces its root back to medieval times, many years before Britain reach a unified nation status (Atkinson et al. 2000). At that time, several local boroughs were governed by royal charter (Atkinson et al. 2000; Chandler 2009). Much of the literature in the studies of local government point out that the LG system in the UK has evolved as a result of having to deal with changes in demographics and living standards brought about by the industrialization process in the larger and more modern cities (Atkinson et al. 2000). In fact, the most significant development in the growth of LG has its origin in the process of industrialization that gathered momentum from the middle of the nineteenth century onwards. This process is said to have brought about a number of complex social and economic problems (Atkinson et al. 2000), all of which were attempts to counter the exigencies of industrialization that produced large movements of population from rural to urban areas. This led to an increased realization among policymakers that they needed to make provisions for the increasing number of industrialized workers and their families in such areas as education, housing, public health, and sanitation (Atkinson et al. 2000). This stage is termed the "first phase limited state" because of a limited range of functions undertaken by the government at that time, as compared with the standards of the early twenty-first century (Tallon 2010). For instance, there was a lack of health-service provision, there was no system of unemployment benefits, and state schools were non-existent.

Now that we have a basic understanding of the history of local government in the UK, we must establish a definition of LG, as it is vital for us to have a working definition of LG before we can consider its structures and functions in the UK. The abundant literature on the general topic (i.e. not specific to Britain) provides many definitions of LG. No one definition is entirely satisfactory simply because there are a number of different types of LG in different countries, each one of them with different characteristics and purposes. For instance, LG characteristics and purposes in the UK differ markedly from its European counterparts, as LG is a component of human rights in most of Europe. However, it is not the aim of this chapter to compare different systems of LG abroad with the British model of LG. Rather, our aim here is to explore the structures and functions of LG in the UK, and that aim is in fact twofold: (1) to explain how LG is arranged constitutionally, and (2) to then consider how LG is funded. The constitutional arrangement and processing of the funding to LG not only renders it to a subservient role, it is also makes it difficult for LAs to develop good, clear policies aimed at exceeding local residents' objectives.

With all that said, let's now define local government in terms of our purposes here. LG in the UK refers to an autonomous entity created by an Act of Parliament. The main purpose of every LG in the UK is to provide local residents with a wide range of social services; every LG and its services are subject to central-government laws (Wilson and Game 2002). That said, LG has other roles which are by no means less important than service provision, such as regulation, strategic planning, advocacy, and promotion (Wilson and Game 2002).

The strength of the definition stated above is that it makes clear that LG in the UK is an autonomous entity created by an Act of Parliament, and as such, it is subject to control and funding by the central government. LG is part of the decentralization process that involves transferring powers from higher levels of governance to lower levels – that is, from central to local government (Pollitt et al. 1998; Crook and Manor 1998; Rondinelli et al. 1989).

Furthermore, we want make clear that local government (LG) is the collective term for local councils (LCs) and/or local authorities (LAs). Therefore, this book uses these three terms interchangeably.

Let's remember that the United Kingdom is a unitary state with an unwritten constitution and a sovereign parliament; it is comprised of four countries: England, Scotland, Wales, and Northern Ireland. All national structures below the central government are regarded as local government. Broadly speaking, there are up to three tiers of LG in the UK: with the top (first) tier is comprised of the regionally devolved LG (Scotland, Wales, and Northern Ireland); the middle (second) tier is comprised of LAs; the bottom (third) tier is comprised of parish councils. The LA second tier is further subdivided into one-tier (unitary) councils and two-tier councils. The upper tiers are normally called county, metropolitan, or city councils, and the lower tiers are called district councils. The tiers are usually represented in the form of a pyramid, as shown in figure 1 (www.gov.uk).

Figure 1. Local-government (LG) pyramid

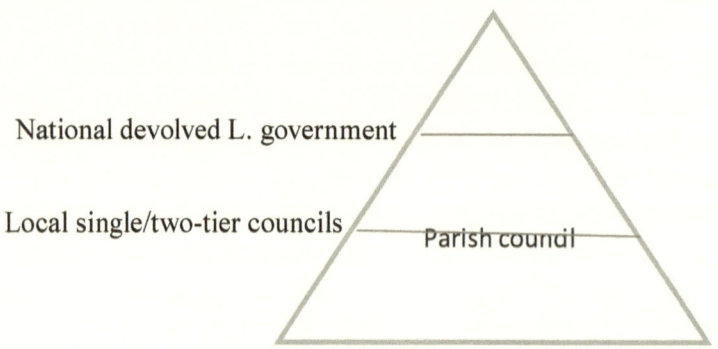

National devolved L. government

Local single/two-tier councils

Parish council

Again, as Leyland (2012) has put it, LG in the UK acts as an agent of the central government, because LG powers are conferred by an Act of Parliament and defined in parliamentary legislation. This implies that LG functions are both mandatory and discretionary (Sawyer 2005). LG has limited ability to raise local taxes, and in many cases LAs are mandated to deliver locally those services that are decided by and subject to central-government supervision (Leyland 2012). That is to say, the central-government minister can insist upon the provision of minimum standards of services.

The current set-up of UK local government is extremely complex for several reasons, primarily the vagueness of Britain's unwritten constitution and the supremacy of Parliament, which implies that local government must comply with central-government directives, and this may not always be in the best interest of local residents. For example, LG is subject to statutory rights that undermine its capacity to pursue policies which will serve local residents' goals (Kingdom 1991). LG also employs various types of elected councils, as well as various types of titles and nomenclature, such as county councils, metropolitan councils, boroughs, and so on. In addition to this, politicians have been able to exploit loopholes in Britain's unwritten constitution and to use this exploitation for their own political gains.

The reorganization and reform process that LG has undergone in recent decades is a prime example of this, in particular, during the

1960s (affecting London), the subsequent partial reorganization that followed in the 1970s (affecting England, Wales, and Scotland), and in the 1980s (again affecting London), all of which were because of ambiguities in Britain's unwritten constitution, combined with parliamentary supremacy, which politicians were able to exploit. As Byrne (2000) has put it, it is also a product of great debates and criticism of the structure of local government. The reorganization and reform of the 1980s, led by the Conservative Party, had more to do with the personality and power of the British Prime Minister at that time, who had a long-standing and deep-seated dislike of local government. The Conservative Party has never regarded local government as constitutionally distinct from central government. In fact, Conservatives perceive LG as merely a part of the public service sector apparatus, which they see as an inefficient body. Conservative policies, then, have been underpinned by the growth of free markets and the rolling back of the state (Hammot 2003). For the Conservative Party, the market, rather than the government, should make the most important decisions in society (Almond et al. 2002).

Furthermore, Byrne (2000) notes that the reorganization and reform of LG in the1990s, as well as in the 2000s, were part of the decentralization process to make public services more efficient and accountable to local residents, which mark out LG as a distinctive form of public administration. Some of the LG reform made by the Labour government in the 2000s was more or less an incremental policy which included more devolution of power to councils in Scotland, Wales, and Northern Ireland, in the form of localism.

As mentioned earlier, LG in the UK has evolved over the centuries because of great debates, criticism, and considerable changes in the Local Government Act of 1972 (affecting England and Wales), 1973 (affecting Scotland), 1963 (affecting London), 1985 (again London), and 2000 (yet again affecting London). Local government in the UK has a clearly defined structure, as described above and depicted in figure 1. LG is comprised of either a unitary system (also known as a one-tier system) or a two-tier system with parish councils (Byrne 2000).

One-tier (unitary) system

The one-tier, or unitary, system refers to a single local authority (LA) responsible for all ranges of local services; it has a geographic boundary that covers the entire urban area (Slack 2003). The unitary system is the main type of LG in Scotland, Wales, and Northern Ireland, and it is the most common system in England. In other words, unitary systems are all-purpose councils, in the sense that they have the power to provide all LG services. Unitary authorities have generally been formed by the merger of two or more lower-tier municipalities within the existing region or by annexation. For example, outer London boroughs that were annexed to the Greater London Council for administrative purposes during the 1960s were formerly part of Essex and Kent.

Since there is only one level of government covering all services for that particular area, there is no need to allocate expenditures among lower levels of government. There is also only one political body to make taxing and spending decisions. One-tier governments could provide a wide range of services. These could be financed from a variety of user fees, charges, and tax sources that would be levied across the metropolitan areas in the same way that the upper tier would finance services in the two-tier model. For example, Boyne (1992) has drawn attention to the fact that having a unitary council can be advantageous because it provides much better service coordination, clearer accountability, more streamlined decision-making, and greater efficiency. Another advantage comes in the form of funding fairness in regard to the provision of services, because there is wider tax base for sharing the costs of services that benefit taxpayers across the region. Slack (2003) observes that the larger taxable capacity of one-tier government increases its ability to borrow and to recover capital and operating costs from user fees. The largest unitary LG can also take advantage of economies of scale in service provision, even though there is some debate as to the validity of the success of a large all-purpose council when it comes to achieving accountability and efficiency in terms of cost savings. For instance, in terms of accountability, Slack (2003) claims that having a large-scale one-tier system of government reduces access and accountability because the jurisdiction becomes too large and bureaucratic. With regard to efficiency, there seems to be little evidence to suggest that merging councils brings cost savings.

Generally speaking, as cited previously, the unitary system is the most common form of LG in the UK. In Scotland, all thirty-two LAs are unitary councils; in Wales, all twenty-two LAs are unitary councils; and in Northern Ireland, all LAs are unitary councils as well. In England, there are three types of unitary authorities: thirty-six metropolitan authorities covering the densely populated urban areas; thirty-three London boroughs; and fifty-seven English shire unitary authorities (www.local.gov.uk).

Nonetheless, the provision of the services described above depend upon whether the council is a one-tier or two-tier council. Unitary councils cover all areas of service provision in their respective localities; whereas the responsibilities in the service provision in two-tier councils vary considerably. [*Please see* table 1 for a list of the responsibilities and functions of the one-tier system council, as well as the services that unitary councils provide.]

Table 1   One-tier (unitary) council responsibilities

Function		**Unitary local council (LC)** **One tier**
Education		X
Housing		X
Social services		X
Highways		X
Transportation		X
Museums and galleries		X
Libraries		X
Strategic planning		X
Economic development		X

Recreation, parks, and sport facilities		X	
Fire services		X	
Food and health inspection		X	
Cemeteries		X	
Markets		X	

Two-tier system

The *two-tier system* refers to the form of urban governance where, in principle, two authorities share the responsibility for service provision. Two-tier systems consist of an upper tier of governance (usually a county council) covering a population of roughly 500,000 to 1.5 million and encompassing its geographic area, and a lower tier of governance (usually a district council) covering a population of about 100,000 and encompassing its geographic area. There are 34 county councils and 238 district councils in England.

The upper tier is responsible for providing the region with wider services, characterized by economies of scale and externalities; whereas the lower tier is responsible for services of local nature (Slack 2003). It noteworthy that there is not any organizational hierarchy between the upper and lower tiers. That is to say, the smaller lower tier of government is not subject to control by the larger upper tier, as both are given a separate range of functions (Chandler 2009). [*Please see* table 2 for the responsibilities and functions of the two-tier system, as well as the services two-tier councils provide.]

Redistribution through a city region is achieved at the upper tier through a combination of tax and spending policies. On the taxation side, tax rates are generally levied uniformly across the region, and the combination of each lower tier LA to the upper-tier municipality depends upon the size of its tax base. That is to say, the larger the LA, the greater its contribution to upper-tier government. On the spending side, the upper-tier government makes expenditures on regionwide services. These expenditures benefit the entire city region and are not necessarily distributed among lower-tier municipalities in the same way that the tax revenues are collected.

Nonetheless, the provision of the services described above depend upon whether the LA is a one-tier or two-tier council. As previously discussed, unitary councils cover all areas of service provision in their respective localities, whereas the responsibilities of service provision in two-tier councils vary considerably.

Two-tier council responsibilities

Function	County council Upper tier	District council Lower tier
Education	X	
Housing	X	X
Social services	X	
Highways	X	
Transportation	X	
Museums and galleries	X	X
Libraries	X	
Planning		X
Strategic planning	X	
Economic development	X	X
Recreation, parks, and sport facilities	X	X
Food and health inspection	X	

Parish councils

Parish and town councils are the lowest level of LG in the UK. Also called the third tier, they are responsible for such services as the management of town and villages centres, litter, cemeteries, parks, ponds, allotments, war memorials, and community halls.

There are around 10,000 such councils in England and Wales, mainly in rural and semi-rural areas (www.demgames.org). Town and parish councils have small budgets and therefore are not subject to the same type of restrictions in funding that one- or two-tier authorities are. This gives the third tier much freedom over how its fund is spent, and because town and parish councils cover much smaller areas, they are often in the best position for involving their local communities in how money is spent. As shown in tables 1 and 2, LAs in the UK are responsible for the management and delivery of education, environmental services, cultural services, police, firefighting, highway maintenance, social services, and so on.

Services provision delivery is no longer the sole responsibility of LAs, as some service provisions and functions are provided by special-purpose districts. These public-funded bodies are also known as quasi-autonomous non-governmental organizations (quangos), and they play a role in the planning provision of the local economy (Fenwick 1996). Although they do not have physical geographic boundaries per se, special-purpose districts are involved in almost every aspect of local and central-government service delivery. However, their operations tend to be concentrated in one area of specialism, either at the central-government or local level, such as regional development agencies (RDAs). The proliferation of special-purpose districts in the UK is said to be a part of the process of decentralization. In order to make the public sector more efficient, the UK central government has for some time turned over the delivery of certain public functions to the quangos described above. More recently, these quangos have simply come to be called extra-governmental organizations (EGOs). There are an estimated 5,500 of these organizations in the UK, of which over 4,700 operate at the local level, and they are said to manage nearly 33.3 per cent of all government expenditures (Amos 1996).

As cited earlier, local government has a variety of characteristics which make it distinct in terms of public administration. One of the most important of all aspects of LG is the role that the Act of Parliament plays in the function and funding of LG.

Local finance

For the most part, local-authority financing has a direct impact on social-services spending, which constitutes a considerable part of the local budget. The UK central government has a substantial influence over LAs by means of financial powers and grants. Most of the gross income of LAs derives from grants paid by the central government, including the redistribution of non-domestic rates, revenue, and capital grants, with the remainder collected locally by such means as council tax, which includes fees, service charges, rents, and capital receipts (www.gov.uk). In fact, about 63 per cent of the gross income of LAs comes from the central government, while the remaining 37 per cent comes from local sources (www.gov.uk).

Details of the full breakdown of the income sources of the LAs in the UK appear in the pages that follow.

Sources of revenue for local authorities (LAs)

Most of LG monies come from grant revenue, which we will discuss later on in this section Grant revenue represents almost half the source of revenue for LAs in the UK. For the purpose of our discussion of how LAs are funded, we first need to understand that LG finance essentially consists of two aspects: the raising of revenue and the expenditures of revenue (Atkinson et al. 2000).

Revenue expenditures refer to all daily spending needed to keep services running; this includes but is not limited to staff wages and salaries, electricity and other utilities, office stationery, schoolbooks, and petrol for council vehicles (Byrne 2000; Atkinson et al. 2000). On the hand, *capital expenditures* refer to such things as the construction of roads and buildings, the purchase of land, and the buying or leasing of large items and equipment (e.g. refuse-collection vehicles).

Revenue expenditures and capital expenditures have two common areas of funding. Firstly, LAs can raise revenue through levying of local taxes in the form of council tax. Secondly, LAs also derive income from business rates and fees and charges. Those vary from

LA to LA, and include charges for such things as home-help services and the use of recreational facilities.

Council tax

Council tax is the system of local taxation in England, Wales, and Scotland; it is used to finance services provided by LCs. It refers to tax imposed on households by LAs in Britain, based on the estimated value of the property and the number of people living in the household (Sawyer 2005).

Again, according to the Valuation Office Agency (VOA), some characteristics of property – size, age, location, and so on – are taken into account when allocating council tax bands. For example, properties in London are far more expensive than any property of the same size and age in in the rest of United Kingdom.

Basically, residents pay council tax to the local council (LC) in which their property is located. A council-tax benefit is available to those on low incomes. This was introduced on 1 April 1993 by the Local Government Finance Act of 1992, as a replacement for the then unpopular community charge (also known as the poll tax), which was a local tax imposed on all residents listed on the register of electors. Council tax rates are set by LAs and are usually expressed as a rate for band D property (www.local.communites.gov.uk). In other words, band D is the government's normal benchmark for comparing council tax in different areas over time. There are eight categories of bands in the UK, and every UK property is allocated to one of them. These eight bands range from A (the lowest) to H (the highest), with D (the middle) as the standard (as mentioned above). Each band is estimated as to its national value on 1 April 1991 (www. voa.gov.uk). This implies that the band for each dwelling in the UK is determined by the market value in which that domestic property falls. These valuation bands determine the amount of council tax that the owner of the property will pay to the LC. For example, one band H property is equivalent to two band D properties, because H pays twice as much tax as D. [*Please see* table 3 for the estimated value of council tax bands in the UK.]

Table 3   Council-tax property band valuation

Band A	£40,000.00	66.7%
Band B	£40,001.00–52,000.00	77.8%
Band C	£52,001.00–68,000.00	88.9%
Band D	£68,001.00–88,000.00	100.0%
Band E	£88,001.00–120,000.00	122.2%
Band F	£120,001.00–160,000.00	144.4%
Band G	£160,001.00–320,000.00	166.7%
Band H	£320,001.00+	200.0%

[Source: VOA]

Fees and sales and service charges

Another source of local financing is that of fees and sales and service charges; this source accounts for 11 per cent of total revenue of LAs in the UK (www.gov.uk). LAs are said to receive substantial revenues from fees service charges for such things as drivers' licences; birth, marriage, and death certificates; parking fines; library (late fees, etc.); motor-vehicle registration; business and professional licences; parking permits; and so on (Byrne,2000).

Government grants and miscellaneous grants

Thus far, we have outlined the main sources of local finance. Having stated earlier in this section that grants comprised the majority of local revenue, now we must turn our attention to explaining the formula that the central government uses to distribute grants to local government. The formula used to allocate funds to LG is very complex and appears to favour LAs with larger populations. Represented in quantifiable terms, the revenue support grant (RSG) for each LA is:

$$RSG + NNDR = SSA - k \text{ tax base}$$

Let us now define the elements of the formula. The *national non-domestic rates* (NNDR), also known as *business rates,* are taxes levied on non-residential properties occupied by companies operating such commercial entities as offices, warehouses, and factories (Sawyer 2005). Firms pay a proportion of the official estimate of the market rent of the properties they occupy. The NNDR is set centrally, but the LAs collect the taxes on behalf of the central government. Generally, NNDRs are collected nationally and allocated to each LA in proportion to population size (Sawyer 2005). That is to say, LAs with bigger populations get a bigger proportion of NNDR revenues, regardless of the LA's tax base.

The *tax base* is a measure of authority for locally levied council tax. *K* is a constant balancing the two sides of the identity. The proportion tax rate is set at 45.8 per cent in England and Scotland, and 45.2 per cent in Wales, and is subject to five-year valuation (www.dfpni.gov.uk).

The lower the tax base of an LA, the higher its RSG. The *revenue support grant* (RSG), the largest grant given by the UK central government, is heavily influenced by population because expenditures in relation to most LA functions increase with larger populations.

The *standard spending assessment* (SSA) is a figure calculated according to a known formula aggregating the measure of spending needs, which is said to ensure that each LA can tax at the same level and provide a standard level of service.

The council tax base is the government's normal benchmark for comparing council tax in different areas over time. The more council tax band D or higher that a council has, the better that council is positioned to face economic difficulties and be less dependent on government financial aid. That said, the amount that a council can raise its council tax is subject to government control, which in turn undermines local councils' capacity to pursue economic goals that exceed local residents' expectations.

Broadly speaking, local tax revenues fall into two main categories: property taxes and non-property taxes. Property taxes include real property (land and physical infrastructure, such as buildings and houses) and personal property (all other property, tangible or intangible; e.g. automobiles, machines, equipment, stocks, and bonds). On the other hand, non-property includes income and sales taxes, and taxes or fees on privileges (e.g. motor-vehicle registration fees, business and professional licences, water and sewage fees). As mentioned above, property taxes continue to be the major source of local revenue, though there has been a measurable shift to non-property revenue sources in recent years (Bland 2002).

Some final thoughts on local finance

What distinguishes LG finance from the monetary affairs of the private sector is, of course, that LG is aimed at providing and maintaining goods and services. In order to achieve these public goods and services, LG must acquire funds from myriad sources, such as taxes, property sales or rentals, various fees and service charges, and debt financing (John and Coles 2000). That said, property tax has always been, and will remain, the mainstay for local revenue. However, sales tax, and special user fees and charges, and income tax (though to a lesser extent) are becoming more widespread alternatives to property taxation.

Even though some responsibilities of LCs are clearly defined, their capacity to act is overshadowed by the profile of the central government in localities. As explained earlier in this chapter, there are essentially two fundamental aspects of local finance: the raising of capital revenue and the expenditure of revenue. Because of this, neighbourhood arrangements and local strategy partnerships are required in order for LAs to meet the targets set by the central government in certain key service areas, and LAs are reliant on the central government to release certain additional regeneration monies. Approximately 63 per cent of LG revenue comes from the central government, thanks to an Act of Parliament which renders LG to a subservient role (Almond 2005).

Again, as previously discussed throughout this book, LG in the UK operates under an unwritten constitution and a sovereign parliament. That is to say, LAs have no choice but to comply with the rules and regulations of the party holding the majority of seats in the Parliament. Turning to Wilson and Game (2002), we find that the lack of a written constitution limits the scope of local government. The vacuum created by the lack of a written constitution often results in the central government imposing stricter restrictions upon LCs that refuse to comply with government wishes. This usually occurs when LCs pursue demonstrably different goals from those of the party in power nationally. In other words, the central government exercises considerable control over the policies of LG.

Nevertheless, it is clear that no matter what systems an LC adopts for raising local revenues, some degree of support from the central government is still required. Atkinson et al. (2000) states clearly that the solution lies in developing a system that strikes an appropriate balance between local autonomy and the exigencies of central government, and that is seen to be fair and impartial. Past experiences have shown it to be a solution that is somewhat elusive. Indeed, lack of spending power and tax raising makes it harder for LG in the UK to develop and choose how much revenue to raise, and how to raise it; and such fiscal autonomy would enable LCs to work better and more efficiently, and would also give them more economic freedom. LG tax rates are set centrally, which makes LAs dependent on the central government for raising revenue to pursue social policies aimed at local people. In short, LG fiscal autonomy (spending power and tax raising) would give LAs the economic freedom to achieve local residents' objectives.

Local authorities (LAs): staff and organization

Local authorities (LAs) are made up of councillors chosen by the members of the community during properly constituted elections. These elected members form the local council (LC), which deliver services and recruits the full-time paid staff of the authority, including engineers, accountants, teachers, clerks, and so on. LCs resemble state civil servants and are organized at the town hall, or county hall, into such departments as education, housing, and social services, among others. LAs perform a variety of service provisions, either directly (provision of schools, homes for elderly people, training centres for people with disabilities, fire service, road building, etc.) or indirectly (through their staffs or by commissioned services from outside organizations). In fact, some of the services provided by outside organizations tend to be concerned with just one field of activity (Byrne 2000); for example, the Arts Council, Food Standards Agency (FSA), Commission of Racial Equality (CRE), and British Broadcasting Corporation (BBC).

In terms of the political composition of each LC, councillors from different political parties make up the full council. The council is divided into individuals groups called committees, which have responsibility for particular services, such as education or planning. Many decisions are recommended by the committees, but they have to be agreed to by the full council. After decisions have been made by the elected members of the council, they are carried by the officer whose job it is to deliver that particular service. Councillors are elected to represent a particular geographical area, which is called a ward. Quite often, there is more than one councillor for every ward. Each councillor has to stand for election every four years. Usually, they are not paid a wage, but they can claim expenses to cover the costs of carrying out their duties.

Each council has a mayor, or a chairman of the council, to undertake ceremonial duties. However, a few councils have elected mayors who provide services. These individuals are elected by the local people, and they each serve for a period of four years. Elected mayors provide political leadership to the council, and they carry out the policies of the LA.

Despite having clear roles and responsibilities, LAs are losing say in how schools and service provisions are run, and must contend with constant interference from the central government on matters of planning; for example, free schools and academies set their own criteria for entry, which hinders early planning. LAs are unable to create new schools to deal with lack of places. Similarly, LAs do not have a say in where schools are built. These are only a few examples amongst many that illustrate how the lack of a written constitution and the supremacy of a sovereign parliament undermine

LG's capacity to pursue policies that meet the expectations of local residents. Still, LG operates within central-government guidelines. Indeed, LAs are subject to central-government statutory rights, with which they must comply. Failure to do so entails much risk for LAs: they could have huge penalties imposed on them or be subject to a partial loss of central-government grants. For example, the central government imposes performance targets on local government as a precondition for allocation of funds, which tend to override any freedom of the LAs.

That said, it should be noted that there is no model of local government that stands above the rest. Different systems of LG have been tried in different shapes and contexts. Indeed, individual cities around the globe have tried different structures at different times and with different results. Consequently, it is very difficult to generalize from examples provided. In other words, the success of appropriate governing structure in any municipality will depend on several factors, such as the nature of the services provided, the revenue sources available, the size and location of the LA, the size of the LC relative to the country as whole, the nature and extent of the central government's presence in the area in terms of financial support and policy priorities, the history of cooperation with neighbouring LAs, and the degree of economic freedom to pursue local residents' goals.

The role of LG has changed in recent years from one of service provision and delivery to one of enabling. Lack of fiscal autonomy reduces the scope of the range of services that LAs can provide and the way in which they can provide it (Booth 2014). The implementation of austerity measures only serves to exacerbate this.

In addition, there are some powerful changes occurring on a global scale that impact the way both central and local government provide services. As a result, LG is coming to play less of a part in direct service provision as the balance between targeted and universal provision shifts. Globalization, with its rapid technological and social changes, is the root cause of many of the powerful and irreversible forces affecting government decision-making processes.

In the next chapter, we will examine how these powerful changes are impacting the relationship between central and local government. We will also explore the effect of globalization and welfare reform on people and localities, including the ways in which globalization processes affect central- and local-government policies and decisions, as well as the extent to which welfare reform is having a detrimental effect on people in the UK.

CHAPTER 4

Globalization and welfare reform

We explored and established the rationale for and the main drivers of austerity measures in chapters 1 and 2, and we analysed the responsibilities, structures and functions of local government in the UK in chapter 3. In this chapter, we will examine the ways in which globalization and other processes linked to it affect central- and local-government decision-making.

It is pertinent to begin with a discussion of what globalization means and encompasses. As are we all aware, at the most general level globalization has come to be associated with myriad definitions; however, for our purposes, we can define *globalization* simply as the process of interconnectedness between societies (Baylis and Smith 2005).

As a result of globalization and rapid technological advances, scholars argue that the world has become smaller, thus creating a global village (Baylis and Smith 2005). Globalization is said to have created an interdependence of governments, with policies increasingly determined or influenced by the perceptions of the impact of globalization (Richard and Smith 2002).

Globalization has had an effect on all aspects of life. Not only has it had an incredible effect on the role and nature of the state internationally, but it has also led to a new layer of governance within countries. Let's explore this more deeply.

A good example of the parliamentary system of government can be seen in Britain, and as a result, when searching for the effects of globalization on the national politics and economy, it would be the first port of call. One fundamental rule of Britain's constitutional arrangement is the legislative supremacy of Parliament; however, since the start of the twenty-first century, parliamentary sovereignty is said to be undermined by the interconnectedness of the world (Richard and Smith 2002). Both governmental and non-governmental institutions have become increasingly involved in cross-boundary networks that are becoming the sites of decision-making and service delivery. Consequently, it has become evident that the state is undergoing a process of hollowing out.

According to Dearlove and Saunders (2000), the term *nation state* refers to a set of institutions – legislative, judicial, and executive – that serve the whole society, with sovereign authority over a defined territory. Richard and Smith (2002) argue that globalization has had a negative impact on what happens within countries because, ultimately, decision-making powers are increasingly being taken away from national governments and given to international governments. This argument can lead to the view that globalization only affects international relations and does not really impact countries, other than regards decisions already made. But this is an oversimplification, particularly in light of the ever-increasing presence of MNCs. This has become a major part of the process of globalization, as both national and local government have been made relatively powerless in the face of global markets and powerful MNCs (Lake 1999). Richard and Smith (2002) go on to state that MNCs are now invested in over 75 per cent of the world trade in manufacturing, and so it has become difficult for the government to control such vast, ever-growing companies, as their importance increases not only in terms of investments, but also in terms of employment and the overall economic growth that make countries dependent upon them (as portrayed in the hollowed-out state thesis).

The hollowing out of the state thesis argues that power is not only being shifted upward from national government to the international, or transnational, arena, but also that it is being drawn away from regional levels in the form of devolution, as is in the case of Britain. Multilevel governance has meant an increase in cooperation among international governments in order to solve domestic and/or international problems (Richard and Smith 2002). For example, there have been rescue plans put into place to bail out Greece, Portugal, Spain, and Ireland, as well as to inject public money to save European, British, and American banks. Nevertheless, the problem with this thesis is that it fails to recognize that globalization does indeed undermine government policy, and central and local policies play a significant role within a country regardless of negative or negligible the input from policy-makers is. Furthermore, this thesis reveals that neo-liberal economic globalization has led to a transformation of the European welfare system on at least three dimensions: most significantly deregulation, privatization, and marketization. In other words, the welfare system has shifted from social justice to economic investment (the productive role of welfare). Such changes, it is argued, may lead to greater risk of social division in terms of poverty and social exclusion (*Journal of Social Policy* 2008).

It is clear from work of Taylor-Gooby et al. (2001) that globalization has had a profound effect on shaping government policies, and also that it played a role in initiating welfare reform in the UK. Generally speaking, the economic, demographic, and labour market shifts are the result of the effect of the process of globalization. The pace of these changes is occurring at lightning speed at the local level, and the ever-changing domestic-service needs are evolving just as rapidly. In addition, service needs are inherently bound together, and all of them are influenced by economic, demographic, social, and political trends and by technological advances. These changes include population, government policies, increases in real incomes, and technology. These factors are the drivers of growth – or shrinkage – in the amount of central-government funding to public service at both the local and national levels (Sawyer 2005)

Indeed, some of these trends especially impact the more vulnerable members of society. The most obvious economic factor is that there has been a rapid increase of those in low-paying jobs, as well as a wider stretch of earnings between skilled and unskilled labour (Broadshaw 1996). In fact, changes in the make-up of earnings, at one end of spectrum, are one result of the increases in the total income of top earners. At the other end of the spectrum, a growing number of households rely solely on cash-transfer benefits caused by increased unemployment and low pay (Platt 2005).

Furthermore, taxation can act as a mechanism for redistribution and as a means for alleviating poverty; however, in recent years, tax policy itself has led to greater inequality and "the combination of direct income tax cuts and indirect tax rises has made it a source of redistribution from poor to rich" (Walker et al. 1997). The decision to end the link between the uprating of some benefits and earnings has ensured that incomes of those attached to the labour market and those dependent on benefits have become increasingly separated (Broadshaw 1996).

Nevertheless, although this policy has saved billions in public expenditure in the short term, it is unsustainable in the long term. The abolition of some cash benefits has had a particularly devastating impact on disadvantaged groups, especially young people and the unemployed. The latter group, to a certain degree, has been the focus of an endless series of measures that has diminished the living standard of them and their families (Broadshaw 1996). Substantial changes have been made to the structure of the welfare system, and these changes affect people and spending in the LAs. Now, the rhetoric of the government is that a combination of natural competition internationally and the policies of deregulation are necessary, as they enable British industry to compete, but they also inevitably lead to an increased dispersion of incomes. However, there is no doubt that the relative increase of dispersion of incomes experienced by people of Britain is either directly linked to policies pursued by government and its failure to respond to the demographic and economic forces that have emerged (Broadshaw 1996).

Furthermore, globalization has brought a massive and ever-increasing global competitiveness; industries and business have been rapidly changing the way they work, and they will have no choice but to continue to do so. Computing and telecommunications are transforming business practices. Some examples of this include corporate downsizing and the emergence of the service industry, which has gained a strong economic position dominated by the manufacturing industry in the past. As a result, all companies have a strong incentive to keep labour costs down. In our supermobile, hyperconnected world, that means jobs that used to be done close to home are moving overseas (or already have done), where wages are lower and workdays are longer. In addition, many of these jobs are now automated, which is cheaper, quicker, and safer. That is to say, machines are doing work previously done by humans, thereby depriving skilled labourers of their livelihoods. Of course, this can, and often does, create social and political instability.

Which brings us to the topic of the demographics in unemployment and other economic problems. The heavy geographic imbalance associated with the recession of the early 1980s and the subsequent recovery only heightened this phenomenon. The trends towards expansion in the technology and service industries favour those cities in the middle and south of England, to the detriment of cities in the north, which rely heavily on the manufacturing and mining industries that have been in continued decline ever since the shift from manufacturing and mining to business (corporate), financial, and information technology (IT) services (Smith 1994). One consequence of this shift has been the creation of spatial imbalances in the economy, with high social costs. We have a country divided by services, with most of business (corporate), financial, and IT jobs (high-paying) concentrated in south, and manufacturing and mining jobs (low-paying) concentrated in the north.

The rapid pace of technological advances has led to changes among consuming patterns too. This is the result of the demographic shift in our population (Smith 1994). Senior citizens, for example, are becoming more and more a major influence in economic markets and financial investments. Population changes within England and Wales in the 1990s were marked by a number of trends; at a regional level, population drift to the south and east England continued, while at a subregional level the picture was one of "counter-urbanization" with city (Barbara 2009).

Other demographic changes have exacerbated poverty, among them, an increase in the number of older people, particularly those who are single and very elderly. Baby boomers who sought to enter the labour force during the recession of the 1980s increased the proportion of families headed by a lone parent as the result of divorce, the breakdown of cohabitation, and the number of children born to unmarried women living alone. Immigration was enabled by cheaper travel costs and encouraged by labour shortages. All these pressures and influences, as well as many others, are having a significant effect on government and domestic policies.

As a result of the many external and internal issues and situations discussed above, welfare reforms in the UK are facing significant challenges that impact their revenue funding structures. Moreover, these challenges will continue to increase, as they are the result of varied conditions, including increases in the real incomes of those at the top of social ladder, stagnant incomes for people in lower-paying jobs, demographic changes, technological changes, and so on. In addition, people are living longer than ever before. The proportion number of older people living in the UK has increased from 1million more men and 0.6 million more women aged 65 or over. The issue of an ageing population and other disadvantaged members of society puts additional pressure on health-care and pension benefits. In fact, the rapid and continuous growth of the urban population not only poses an additional threat to local government, in terms of service provision, but also to national government, in terms of responding to the higher demands of an increased population stretching the government welfare bill further than ever before.

In the foregoing discussion, we have emphasized the way in which globalization processes have transformed the way nation states operate, which in turn has caused a profound effect on welfare reform. The advantages of bringing people together in a supermobile, hyperconnected world include the reduced cost of production. However, there is a link between globalization and welfare reform which in turn has an effect on individuals. This is often overlooked, but this chapter seeks to emphasize the significance of this link.

Let's first consider that companies tend to move to countries or places where labour is cheaper and taxes are more generous. Competition at the global level only increases this trend. This principle of competition also applies within LAs in the UK, which are often compelled to compete with one another for resources at all levels. Globalization, again, has exacerbated this. The pace and scale of the globalization process has impacted the way services are delivered, provided, and perceived. The very nature of most of work done in the past has changed because process of globalization. For example, jobs that were once done by many people are now done by machines, as previously mentioned. Globalization, combined with technological advances, led to the decline of the manufacturing industry, formerly a major source of employment for many families in Scotland, Wales, and north-east and north-west England. This decline led to mass unemployment in those regions. In some areas, those jobs were replaced, but they were all low-paying jobs.

The social-security safety net in the UK was created to help people who were unemployed by keeping them from falling into the poverty trap. Social security has been a core tenet of British society, but it has been eroded by the changes brought about by the Welfare Reform Act of 2012, which imposes a cap on social payments to each household. Research undertaken by Oxfam and the New Policy Institute in 2014 found that cuts in housing benefits and changes to council-tax support has left around 1.75 million of the poorest families worst off, by having a shortfall in their incomes as a result of the social-security reform that limit payments to social benefits.

The Welfare Reform Act of 2012 also imposes tighter conditions on benefit entitlements, which certainly exacerbates the living conditions of the people dependent upon those benefits. There is clear evidence that tighter eligibility conditions are not having the intended effect; in fact, they are creating severe hardship for increasing numbers of people.

People receiving jobseeker's allowance (JSA) and employment support allowance (ESA) have to comply with a number of criteria as conditions for receiving their social-security payments: for example, applying for a certain number of jobs weekly, attending meetings at the jobcentre, and being available for work. Failure to comply with these criteria may result in the issuance of sanctions or penalties, which in turn can lead to delayed or withdrawn payment. What is more, since the changes were implemented in October 2012, more than 1 million sanctions have been applied, with 20 per cent of these imposed on people with disabilities (www.truselltrust.org).

It is the view of Trussell Trust (www.trusselltrust.org 2014) that the increased number of people inappropriately sanctioned is the result of a combination of various factors intrinsically linked to quick-fix policy intentions designed to get the economy back on track. These factors include the pace at which changes are instituted, the poor guidance provided for dealing with the changes, and the lack of support and training for jobcentre staff, combined with redundancies at the Department for Work and Pensions (DWP).

What is not easy quantifiable is the extent to which welfare reform impacts people, given its stages of introduction and the mobile nature of the population. We live in globalized world where what happens in one country affects other countries and other parts of the world. There is a clear link between globalization and welfare, in the sense that the process of globalization has changed the very nature of the way we work, live, commute, and communicate, as well as the way in which incomes are distributed. Globalization has made travelling cheaper and more accessible (i.e. it has made migration easier), and it has brought advances in medicine which make us living longer. All these factors have contributed to changes in demographics among the population, and this has put additional pressure on state finances. That said, it is possible to characterize households that are likely to experience a very significant shortfall in income.

The full extent to which the Welfare Reform Act 2012 affects people will be analysed in the next chapter. Having said that, there are some attributes that every LA needs in order to be successful, such as the nature of service it provides to its population, its size, its location, the revenue available to it, and its degree of economic freedom. These attributes play a vital role in comparing the extent to which austerity measures impact on LG; indeed, they represent the key factor necessary for assessing the extent to which cuts to public spending affect people and impact the day-to-day running of LAs.

Chapter 5

Austerity: cure or curse?

Before we begin to compare and contrast arguments about the impact of austerity measures in two specific local authorities in the UK, we need to understand what is happening to individuals and localities. Our aim in this chapter is to assess the impact of austerity measures on people and local government, and then evaluate whether austerity measures are having the desired and intended effect.

The impact of austerity measures on individuals

As argued in previous chapter, austerity measures were implemented by the coalition government primarily as an attempt to show international creditors that the UK has a long-term plan to rescue her economy and fulfil her economic obligations following the huge credit crisis and global recession of 2008–09. Therefore, the coalition government set out in its 2010 budget to reduce the public deficit by 70 per cent of GDP by the fiscal year 2014–15, and also to retain the UK's AAA-plus economic status. However, the coalition government failed to achieve both those goals. Firstly, the coalition government missed its original target of reducing the public deficit which stands stubbornly at 74 per cent of GDP. Secondly, attempts to retain Britain's AAA-plus economic status suffered a massive blow when Fitch, a rating agency, stripped the UK of that long-held status.

Again, the austerity measures in the UK adopted by the coalition government were intended to reduce public spending. Consequently, these measures brought several changes that not only had a significant impact on the way that social benefits are provided and delivered, but also added a considerable strain on the finances of the people on low incomes. Thus, we can see that of the many changes brought by the austerity measures imposed by the coalition government, welfare reform is a pertinent one, particularly the way in which entitlement to social benefits now works. For instance, entitlement to the housing benefit has been cut, and council-tax support has been reduced. Above all, the Welfare Reform Act 2012 has meant switching from several benefits (means tested) to only one benefit (universal credit), which now has tighter eligibility criteria. The overall result of these changes has been one of severe negative impact on individuals in the UK.

This certainly applies to housing, considering that the UK has the highest housing-cost levels in Europe, with people spending on average 40 per cent of their income on rent or a mortgage (*The Guardian* 2012). In addition, there is a chronic shortage of housing supply because construction of homes is low; thus, many people have applied for social housing. The number of families on a waiting list for social housing is estimated to be around 1.8 million, and while they are waiting for social housing, these families are renting privately (*The Guardian* 2012).

Housing costs have risen sharply, especially for renters in the private sector, with rents increasing by 67 per cent between 2002–03 and 2011–12. Renting costs are rising twice as much as income levels, to the point where average rents are unaffordable in almost half of England's LAs. The cost of housing is even more severe, with rents at 7.6 per cent, higher than anywhere else in the UK. This figure shows that people in London are bearing the brunt of the new welfare cap, which reduces payments for households to £26,000.00 per year. London households are likely to see their payments reduced by £100.00 per week (or more), largely as a result of the cap on the housing benefit, which limits payment for a one-bedroom property to £250.00 per week, rising to £400.00 per week for a four-bedroom house.

The number of working people who need housing benefits to make ends meet has increased more in London than anywhere else in the UK. According to NIESR, the number of employed individuals in Britain claiming benefits rose from 652,000 in May 2010 to more than 1 million in 2013, an increase of approximately 59 per cent (NIESR Report, 2014; also cited in *Evening Standard*).

Furthermore, other policies brought by the coalition government have led to massive job losses in both the public and private sectors, as well as pay freezes and partial or total withdrawal of services. Suffice it to say that policies brought by the coalition government have impacted negatively individuals in the UK. For instance, reduction in the social services has led to a decrease in levels of social services in both public and private service provision. Access to social services for vulnerable people, such as people with disabilities, is a prime example of this. The allowance for these individuals appears to have been considerably reduced and made difficult to access by introduction of tighter eligibility criteria, as compared to allowance and access prior to the global economic crisis and recession.

What is more, staff reduction in local councils has clearly impacted service delivery, as well as the availability of and access to social services. One consequence of staff shortage is that there is less individualized time available for service users, another is that there is additional pressure on the fewer professionals who are available, with significant changes to their workday patterns. That is to say, they are working longer days and more hours in order to meet the higher demand and increased needs of benefits users. Because LAs have less money available to spend, they are forced to do more with less money, which of course puts increased pressure on staff. This is true at all levels of bureaucracy. For example, redundancy of staff has seen an increase to the timescale for issuing passports to new applicants and for renewing existing passports. Local residents must wait longer to receive calls, communications (letters and e-mails), and responses to queries.

In terms of unemployment, the full impact of recent growth has not fed through. Jobs losses are still significant, with a rise in unemployment of 6.6 per cent in April 2014, as compared to the low unemployment rate of 5.2 per cent in September 2007. Low-skilled workers with little education are the ones most affected, particularly young people, BME, and women. The rate of unemployment among young people between the ages of 18 and 24 remain at an all-time high of over 950,000 (ONS 2014).

As far income is concerned, the policy adopted by the coalition government has clearly impacted people's incomes. The average household income fell in real terms, and the cost of living continues to rise. The incomes of low-skilled and less-educated individuals fell the most dramatically. In addition, changes to the eligibility criteria for receiving benefits, along with the total withdrawal of certain benefits in some cases, have made a bigger impact on the relative living standards of those who have lost their jobs or who rely on welfare benefits, because the government has imposed several cuts to public funds. These cuts include reductions to housing benefits, child tax credits, and disability benefits, as well as changes to council-tax support, all of which puts more strain on families.

Ever since welfare benefits have been enforced in April 2011, approximately 780,000,00 of the poorest families have experienced a shortfall in their housing benefits, and continue to do so (www. trusselltrust.org). The welfare reform is said to have created severe hardships for increasing numbers of people, with the abolition of social funds in 2013 considered to be one of numerous policies changes causing further hardship to low-income households. Previously, families and individuals could apply for interest-free hardships loan that would be paid back through their social security benefits. Tighter eligibility criteria for receiving those funds has led people to turn to loan sharks and payday loan agencies. Furthermore, the excessive cuts to or reduction of benefits has driven the poor out of London because of the high cost of living. Cuts to family working-tax credits have forced thousands of families rely on food banks. The number of food banks and payday loan companies are said to be growing faster than ever before, as a result of the combination of factors described throughout this chapter.

According to the Trussell Trust (Britain's largest food-bank donor), the number of people on referral for assistance increased from 12 per cent in 2011–12 to 18 per cent during the period of April to September 2013. Of the referrals between April and June 2013, 52 per cent were to the result of problems with social security (www.truselltrust.org). The driving factors leading people to seek referrals to food banks are the changes to social-security payments, low incomes, bedroom-tax charges, reduction in council-tax support, the abolition of social funds, and the increase in social-security sanctions.

The growing numbers of people relying on food banks and people in debt further illustrates that austerity is a dangerous idea, and it is not working. Despite all government rhetoric and the positivism of economists and politicians alike, the truth is that individuals are and will remain significantly worse off than they were in 2007, thanks to the high cost of living. The rising living cost has placed a strain on people's incomes since the recession, greatly reducing the purchasing power of many households, particularly those at the lower end of the income scale. One reason for given for this is that wages have lagged behind prices, particularly with the high increase in the cost of essentials, such as transportation, petrol, food, and energy. That is to say, people on low incomes have less money to pay for the bare necessities. Another reason is that the nature of employment has changed, with more and more people failing to find full-time jobs which would qualify them for the benefits and protection given to full-time employees (Hilton 2014; also cited in *Evening Standard*). Having said that, it is not hard to see why people are worse off than they were in 2007. The economic recovery has yet to fill the pockets of ordinary people. Further evidence of discontentment with austerity measures shows up in the political arena. Many recent local and elections across Europe and in the UK saw the main political parties failing to hold a majority for the first time in more than century. Simply stated, austerity is not working.

What is often absent from the debates of austerity measures' impact on people is the naturally cyclical nature of the economy. That is to say, the economy works in cycles which are normally susceptible to ups (expansion) and downs (recession or contraction), and these ups and down can be determined by several factors domestically and internationally. Because of this, arguments put forward by proponents of austerity measures are at best dubious and at worst a demonstrably dangerous idea. Philippe Legrain, a former adviser to the President of the European Commission (EC), claims that "the EU institution has become an instrument for creditors to impose their will on debtors"(*Financial Times* 2014). From the bulk of literature on the topic, it clearly seems entirely appropriate to attribute the idea of embarking on austerity measures as an activity more based on ideology than established fact. The main motive is seeking the greatest return on creditors' investment.

The impact of austerity on local government (LG)

The most extraordinary consequence of public-expenditure restraint has been in LG funding, so welfare reform is a pertinent issue for LAs. As we have seen, there have been dramatic changes in welfare reform. The central government has introduced these changes, some of them more or less independently of changes to the labour market and demographic structure, but all of them have exacerbated the living conditions of ordinary people, and will continue to do so. In terms of local government, LG accounts for 23 per cent of public-sector expenditure in the UK, collectively, and is one of the largest sources of employment in England, which has 1.7 million full-time equivalent staff. The majority of these individuals are in administration and other support services. In fiscal year 2011–12, LG expenditure accounted for 48 per cent of all LG service expenditure (www.gov.uk). These numbers illustrate how a reduction in LG funds and staff will always have a detrimental effect on service provision to local residents.

Despite the signs of a positive national economic outlook, public services will continue to face tough financial challenges over the next few years. As cited earlier, one of the key features of LG in the UK is the centralization of power in Whitehall (Westminster), with regard to the funding of LAs. Local government gets most of its money from central government. In fact, 63 per cent of local expenditure comes from national-government funding, most of which is determined by a centrally decided formula which distributes the RSG to each LA. As discussed previously, the central government has the power to limit the total amount that LAs spend, and to a great extent, the central government also determines how LAs spend that money. Grants to LAs account for approximately 25 per cent of total expenditure. Council tax only makes up 17 per cent of what LAs spend. So cuts to the money LCs receive from central-government grants are substantial enough to create large a difference in LC spending power. In other words, cuts to central-government grants really impact what LAs can afford. Therefore, cuts to public expenditures have brought fundamental changes to the way that LCs spend money. Councils usually allocate money to each service and then look for savings within those areas of spending. This way of allocating money always gave council departments stability and continuity, but in some cases led to duplication and waste. In order to fully grasp what happens when LAs are faced with cuts over long periods, we need to consider the whole structure of the LAs and how they work on behalf of local residents. [*Please see* chapter 3 for details.]

Unfortunately, tackling this huge challenge means that some people in some LAs will miss out. What is more, LAs have the legal responsibility to provide certain services; however, the provision of some services has been subject to changes, caps, and/or reductions in order to comply with directives from the central government. Compliance is mandatory, as LAs are required by law to set a balanced budget, which implies cuts to many services in order to balance the books. Thus, we can see that austerity measures impact LG in a variety of ways; it is not a single, unified causal process, but, rather, the effect of other national and international developments. Consequently, the response to this experience will, indeed, vary from LA to LA.

A research study carried out by scholars at Sheffield Hallam University measured the impact of cuts in spending power on individual LAs, during the period of 2010 to 2015. Researchers based their calculations on two key principles. One was looking at the local caseload of claimants, and the other was studying the official impact assessment of the likely losers. The research concluded that inner London boroughs would be most affected by restrictions on housing benefits, because of the high housing costs (both rents and mortgages); whereas the traditional industrial heartland areas of England, Scotland, and Wales would be hard hit be other factors, particularly the tighter eligibility criteria for disability benefits (*Financial Times* 2013).

For example, the total annual impact of the household benefit cap on the London Borough of Hackney would be £5 million, while the annual impact on the Royal Borough of Kensington and Chelsea (K&C) would be £4 million. The overall amount of money, in terms of spending power, that these two LAs would likely lose when accounting for the cuts to other social benefits, such as child benefits, disability allowance, and incapacity benefits would be: London Borough of Hackney, £119 million; the Royal Borough of Kensington Chelsea (K&C), £62 million (*Financial Times* 2013).

Given this evidence, it can be argued that, at least to some extent, the austerity measures have exacerbated living conditions for some people and have had a detrimental effect on LG. What is more, they will likely continue to do so. The effect and magnitude of austerity measures proved to be costly to Britain's main political parties in the last local elections. The Conservative Party lost several safe councils, while we have seen a surge in the number of people voting for far-right parties in European elections. Thus, it is noteworthy that the political composition of the LA and the degree of local bureaucratic strength, rather than the need for service and the availability of resources, are more likely to have a considerable effect on different levels of expenditures, as well as having a bearing on policy outcomes (Ashford 1978). It is the view of the Conservative Party that LA tax should be restrained; therefore, it should be kept as low as possible (Elcock 1994). LCs should confine themselves to meeting statutory rights and supporting voluntary groups while embracing few worthy causes. For Conservatives, it is the obligation of all citizens to be responsible for making their own provisions and support, instead of relying on the LA to provide them (Elcock 1994). The Labour Party, in contrast, believes that services must be provided to all citizens who need them and that such expenditures help the needy in the society (Elcock 1994). This partially explains the Conservative Party's willingness to embark on austerity measures. However, the pace in which cuts have been done by the coalition government hasn't given LAs much room to manoeuvre or to plan any good strategy for dealing with huge cuts to their local budgets. A more progressive cut would have given them more time and room to minimize the loss of revenue and look at better ways to innovate the provision and delivery of services, while simultaneously reducing services and staff. In today's more fragmented landscape of service provision, it becomes harder for LAs to meet the expectations of hard-working families in a consistent way across the country. With a second round of massive cuts from the central government scheduled to come into effect in April 2015, the financial situation of LAs looks very bleak. However, it is clear that cutbacks were implemented because of particular national economic and political choices (Sykes et al. 2001). As we mentioned in previous chapters, these choice are ideologically driven. In fact, it is people rather than states that make decisions to change or introduce policies (Sykes et al. 2001), and this process usually involves both political and ideological choices.

In the next chapter, we will take a closer look at the effect that some of these political and ideological choices have on LAs. Specifically, we will examine two LAs – the London Borough of Hackney and the Royal Borough of Kensington and Chelsea (K&C) – in order to determine the extent to which people in these two LAs are coping with the reduction of public expenditure.

CHAPTER 6

The tale of two boroughs: a comparative study of UK local authorities (LAs)

It is aim of this chapter to explore the extent to which austerity measures impact LAs in UK. To do so, we will undertake a comparative study of two LAs, as mentioned in the preceding chapter. These two LAs are the London Borough of Hackney and the Royal Borough of Kensington and Chelsea (K&C), which we will refer to as Hackney and K&C, respectively throughout the rest of this chapter.

Before we proceed, must establish an understanding of the goal and purpose of comparative analysis (study), the traditional focus of which is to examine similarities and dissimilarities. In fact, throughout this analysis we will focus on marginal or absolute changes in the levels of local public spending and service provision in the two LAs (Hackney and K&C), paying particular attention to the similarities and dissimilarities among those changes. For instance, one LA, Hackney, is controlled by the Labour Party; the other LA, K&C, is controlled by the Conservative Party. Furthermore, we are going to look at the impact of welfare reform at the local level, in terms of variations in pattern of spending in each borough, its characteristics and impacts on the people in the two LAs, as well as the reasons for variations in the levels of spending cuts between them. We are working with assumptions that these cuts will be felt differently and vary from place to place, or region to region, throughout the UK, but, again, our comparative analysis only focuses on the two LAs, Hackney and K&C.

In order to more fully consider the two LAs that are the subject of our study, let's examine them more closely. Hackney and K&C are both unitary LCs located in England, and both are urban inner London boroughs. We have chosen to focus on English LAs, particularly in London, because London's system of local government has a markedly different feature from LG in the rest of the country. Simply put, London is the capital city of the UK, the engine of the nation's economy, and the most diverse and populous city in country. So, using these two urban LAs in London, we are going to the compare differences and similarities between them, using concepts that are applicable in more than one case. We are trying to see whether (or not) the patterns of observed variations are consistent with our theoretical expectations. For example, will examine the characteristics of each borough in terms of its local councillors, its political convictions/affiliations, its population's demographic composition, its geographical location, its local residents' degree of participation or engagement in political process, its level of resilience when faced with adversity, its local councillors' ability to lobby the central government and to have great connections with and within the incumbent government, and so on. Any of these characteristics may impact disadvantaged people in one LA more than those in another. Our analysis will take all these considerations into account.

Now, before we take a closer look at these two LAs in order to compare the impact of austerity measures upon the people living in these two UK localities, we need to establish some background information. As mentioned earlier, Hackney and K&C are both urban LAs in London. More specifically, each is a unitary council, each is one of thirty-three boroughs that form the Greater London Authority (GLA). The GLA is divided into inner and outer London boroughs. The inner London boroughs refer to LCs that were part of the former

London city county area. The outer London boroughs are formed by areas of Essex, Hertfordshire, Middlesex, Kent, and Surrey, which were transferred to the GLA in 1969 for administrative purposes. The GLA is responsible for providing citywide government throughout London, with special responsibility for police, fire, strategic planning, and transportation (www.demsgames.org). With a more than 7 million inhabitants, London is by far the most populous city in the UK; it is also the biggest contributor to the nation's GDP, with 45 per cent.

Back to our key examples, Hackney and K&C have marked differences in demographic composition of households, ideological perspectives, territorial density, and economic status. Thus, we believe that the extent to which austerity measures impact people at the local level in the these two unitary LAs may lie in the size and profile of the local population and political affiliations, along with the local welfare needs and demands for services in each LA.

As stated above, Hackney is an inner London borough within the GLA. Hackney has a remarkably diverse population, with an estimated 252,119 inhabitants; of this number, 125,117 are males, representing 47 per cent of the population, and 127,002 are females, representing 53 per cent of the population (ONS 2011). Hackney's population density is approximately 11,476 residents per square kilometre. Hackney is ranked as the second-most deprived LA in England, after Liverpool (ONS 2010). The population is ethnically diverse, as mentioned previously. Of the resident population, 89,450 (41%) describe themselves as white British, 30,978 (14%) are in the other white group; BME represent 41.5 per cent of the population (GLA 2011).

Since 1997, Hackney has been governed by the Labour Party, whose policies differ markedly from those of the Conservative Party. What is more, the services industry is the principal source of employment in Hackney, representing around 92.0 per cent of the borough's jobs; finance, IT, and other business follow at 32.5 per cent; next comes public administration, health, and education, at 28.7 per cent; after that, distribution and hotel and restaurant, at 15.2 per cent; followed by transportation and communication, at 9.0 per cent; after that, other services, at 6.2 per cent; and, finally, manufacturing, at 5.6 per cent (www.nomis.co.uk). In regard to occupations, the majority of Hackney residents are in professional occupations, representing approximately 29.0 per cent of employment in the borough, followed by associated professional and technical occupations, which represent 22.0 per cent (www.nomis.co.uk). In 2010–11, 69.0 per cent of working-age residents of Hackney were employed (www.dwp.gov.uk). That rate is higher than average for London, which stands at 68.2 per cent. The employment rate in Hackney is higher among men (74.4%) than women (64.0%) (www. Hackney.gov.uk).

K&C is also an inner urban London borough within the GLA, but as described above, K&C is a Royal borough. K&C has a relatively small population – estimated 158,300 inhabitants – as compared to Hackney (252,119). Of the K&C population, 78,100 are males and 80,200 are females (ONS 2011). The borough has the highest population density of any LA in England and Wales, with more than 13,000 residents per square kilometre (ONS 2001). BME represent over 21 per cent black, of which 3.7 per cent are of African origin. While 50 per cent are white British, a further 28 per cent are from other white ethnic groups (www.neighbourhood.statistics.gov.uk).

Unlike Hackney, K&C is one of wealthiest LAs in England, and it has some of the most expensive real estate in the world (GLA 2011). The borough is governed by the Conservative Party, whose ideological view is distinctly different from that of the Labour Party. This is another major difference between Hackney and K&C. As we've already remarked upon K&C real estate, let's extend the discussion to housing, which illustrates the differences between the two boroughs quite effectively. Much of K&C council housing is privately owned (43.8%), and a great majority of its inhabitants are employed in the service industry (94.1%). Distribution follows, at 35.4 per cent; next come IT and finance, at 24.3 per cent (ONS 2011). Despite being the richest borough in the country, K&C has a wide extreme of affluence and poverty (www.news.bbc.co.uk). In fact, this LA is one of most polarized boroughs in London. Just over half of its benefits recipients live in one quarter of its neighbourhood. The quarter of least-deprived areas in K&C has only 5 per cent of benefits recipients. This is in sharp contrast with Hackney, where even the least-deprived quarter has 20 per cent of benefits recipients, and the most-deprived quarter has just over 30 per cent (New Institute Policy 2012). K&C has the lowest proportion of low-paid people in London (approximately 9% of K&C residents); whereas Hackney has a higher proportion of low-paid people (approximately 20% of Hackney residents) (New Institute Policy 2012). In 2010, average gross weekly pay received by Hackney residents was £583.00, slightly below the K&C average and also below the London average of £609.00.

So far in this chapter, we have considered the similarities and dissimilarities between our two example LAs, Hackney and K&C, both in London. We have highlighted the differences in population size and profiled both local populations, including such conditions as employment, housing, and benefits recipients.

The next point is to examine more closely the number of working-age people claiming benefits among the residents of Hackney and K&C. Approximately 37 per cent of young people in Hackney live in households dependent on benefits, and approximately 46 per cent of inhabitants under the age of 20 live in overcrowded households. Among them, young people of BME origin represent 56.5 per cent, and white young people represent 43.5 per cent (GLA 2012).

Our next point is to try to find a correlation between those residents needing benefits and the effect that cuts in spending (i.e. austerity measures) have had on those individuals. In order to do this, we will consider the number of people in both Hackney and K&C claiming key benefits, the key services needed among people of working age, and the reduction to the public expenditure – that is, the effect of welfare reform on the disadvantaged people in our two LAs. Figure 2 reveals the connection between the economy and employment trends and central-government policies and budgetary discretion, as well as the way in which they affect key services and key benefits, which in turn impact disproportionally upon ordinary people – especially those with disadvantages.

Table 4   Number of working-age people claiming key benefits
Hackney Number Percentage K&C Number Percentage

Claimants s of benefit	31.420	17.9%	11.690	10.2%
Job seekers	9.870	5.5%	2.930	2.6%
Incapacity benefits	13.660	7.7%	6.090	5.3%
Lone parents	3.450	1.9%	900	0.8%
Carers	1.950	1.1%	700	0.6%
Disabled	1.900	0.8%	580	0.5%
Other income benefits	880	0.5%	390	0.3%
Key out work benefits	27.860	15.6%	10.310	9%

[Data as of February 2013. Source:]

Figure 2. Connection between people, local government, and
central government

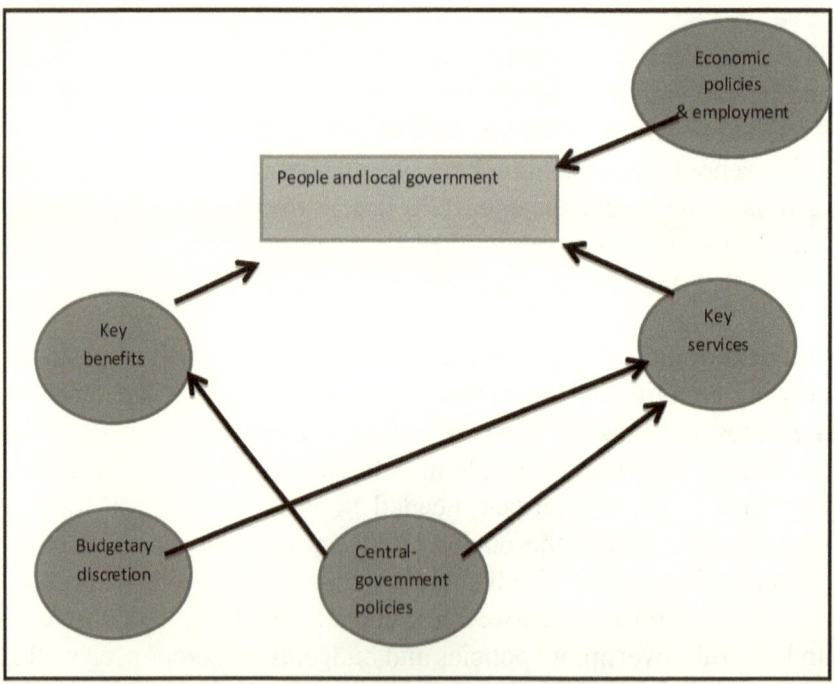

Table 4 shows that Hackney has a higher proportion of residents claiming key benefits, as compared to K&C. Nevertheless, figure 2 shows how the combination of the economy, tighter spending, and central-government policies affects key benefits and key services, which in turn impact people (especially the disadvantaged). By analysing figure 2 and table 4, we can see that the people in Hackney will be worse off than the people in K&C. In other words, in terms of our two example LAs, the impact of austerity measures will be felt more acutely in Hackney than in K&C.

Two main reasons account for this. Firstly, the constitutional arrangement in which LG operates in UK requires LAs to meet targets set by the central government. Secondly, LAs lack the power to set their own local tax, which in turn affects their capacity to pursue policies that are better suited to local people. In other words, LAs are compelled to comply with targets set by the central government in order to get access to government funds and grants. Therefore, LA spending is affected by central-government policies. For example, the switch from housing benefit to universal credit has had a profound impact on LAs' expenditure (as shown in tables 5 and 6). A significant variation in the patterns of benefits expenditure in the two LAs (as shown in tables 5 and 6) is the result of central-government policy changes with regard to eligibility for JSA, incapacity benefit, housing benefit, and other income-related benefits (DWP and OBR 2013).

**Table 5   Benefit expenditure per year –
London Borough of Hackney**

	2009–10	2010–11	2011–12	2012–13
	£608.20	£638.8	£663.8	£545.5
Incapacity Benefit	15.2	13.7	12.6	
Council Benefit	33.5	35.2	35.5	
Caregiver Allowance	6.3	6.7	7.6	
Housing Benefits	244.2	266.7	283.7	
Lone Parents	25.1	21.4	18.2	
JSA	28.7	31.3	35.2	
Income Support	71.7	65	57	

[Source: DWP revenue returns 2012–13]

Table 6   Benefit expenditure per year –
Royal Borough of Kensington and Chelsea (K&C)

	2009–10	2010–11	2011–12	2012–13
	£362.40	£378.8	£385.7	£338.3
Incapacity Benefit	8.3	7.8	7	
Council Benefit	13.5	14.1	13.6	
Caregiver Allowance	2.4	2.6	2.9	
Housing Benefits	139.7	150	152.9	
Lone Parents	7.5	6.5	5.3	
JSA	10.8	11.1	11	
Income Support	29.1	27.1	23.3	

[Source: DWP revenue returns 2012–13]

Let's remember that the economy is cyclical. On the one hand, there are periods of sustained high spending when the economy is growing. On the other hand, there are periods of low spending when the economy is on a downturn. Consequently, these factors must be taken into account by policymakers when making choices. That said, overall central-government policies – such as fiscal (economic), employment, access to key benefits and services, and so on – have numerous repercussions on people and LAs.

Our two example LAs of Hackney and K&C illustrate this. Tables 5 and 6 show the increases in public expenditures in the two LAs, tduring the period of 2009 to 2012, and then a decline in expenditures during the 2012–13 fiscal year. The increase of public expenditures during the period of 2009 to 2012 was the result of the surplus of the economy during the years before the recession, whereas the decrease in public expenditures was to the result of the shrinking of the economy.

**Table 7   Number of households renting in social housing –
Hackney and K&C**

Council (Local Authority)[1][2] *Households Count Mar11 Households Count Mar11*	7,201	439,727	2,079,778	24,163
Social Rented; Rented from Council (Local Authority)[1][2] *Households Percentage Mar11 Households Percentage Mar11*	9.2	13.5	9.4	23.8
Private Rented; Private Landlord or Letting Agency[1][2] *Households Count Mar11 Households Count Mar11*	26,676	775,591	3,401,675	28,112
Private Rented; Private Landlord or Letting Agency[1][2] *Households Percentage Mar11 Households Percentage Mar11*	34.0	23.7	15.4	27.6

[Source: ONS]

Having looked at patterns of variation among numbers of claimants in our two example boroughs (LAs), let's now explore the extent to which current changes to policies – specifically welfare reform – are impacting people in Hackney and K&C. Again, by looking at the pertinent statistics and information we may sense that welfare reform is having a more detrimental effect on residents in Hackney than in K&C. Statistics from 2010–11 reveal that there was an increase in the number of households in privately rented accommodations that received benefits in the amount of £10,000.00 to 12,000.00. This is reflected in changes in the monthly profile of access to housing benefits and to universal credit, which affects payments. Primarily, it reflects modest growth in income tax and National Insurance contributions (NICs) (OBR 2013). The increase in spending was largely because of the increasing amount of people claiming JSA and falling in the numbers of unemployed. In April were down to 31.3 per cent on a year earlier. Conversely, it remained unchanged in K&C during the same period (ONS 2013). The evidence seems to be strong that changes to housing benefits could exacerbate a situation already made worse by the hardships faced as a result of London's high housing costs (rents and mortgages).

To explore the similarities and dissimilarities between the two LAs even further, let's examine other benefits. In the larger sense, welfare reform and the central-government policy changes currently reducing public services have a significant negative impact on residents in Hackney. According to the rating agency Standard & Poor (S&P 2009), the negative impact on people in Hackney can be viewed as the greater reliance on the broad range of public services by Hackney residents, as compared to residents of K&C, an affluent neighbourhood with a small proportion of disadvantaged people. Furthermore, most households in K&C have the capacity to supplement public benefits with other forms of provision. This includes single people aged 20 to 35, families requiring housing with 5 or more bedrooms, and households paying rents above the new local housing allowance threshold of 30 per cent. Nonetheless, the two LAs current expenditure increased. Hackney's net expenditure increased from £608.2 in 2010 to £663.8 .8 in 2012, and then fall to £545.5 during fiscal year 2012–13. On the other hand, K&C's net expenditure grew from £362.4 in 2010 to £385.7, and then fell to £338.3 during fiscal year 2012–13 (www.dwp.gov.uk). This represents a great decline if compared with the period of 2010 to 2012. This decline does not result primarily from decreases in incomes but from a remarkable decrease in spending power. It is also believed coincide with a change in timing of the payments of grants from the central government to LAs (OBR 2013).

Another reason given for the variation in the benefits expenditure in the two LAs shown in tables 5, 6, and 7 is the changes to the overall benefits system. For example, from late 2008 until mid–2011, the changes in eligibility rules for lone-parent income support resulted in fewer lone parents (predominantly women) being able to claim that benefit, which in turn resulted in more lone parents (again, predominantly women) claiming JSA while looking for jobs (www.dwp.gov.uk). The welfare reform legislation brought changes that saw every lone parent in the country with a youngest child aged 7 or over switch their income support to JSA (www.gov.uk). As a result, there was, and still is, a surge in the number of working-age people claiming out-of-work benefits. The figures show a slight difference in term of percentages of people affected in the two LAs. Moreover, the figures appear to reveal that austerity measures are negatively impacting residents of Hackney, as compared to residents of K&C. This is the result of substantial differences in the composition of households, the status of employment and types of occupations, gender, ethnicity, qualifications, and levels of education attainment among the people in the two boroughs. Hackney has a higher proportion of BME, young people, and single women, as compared to K&C. Hackney also has a higher proportion of people in low-paying jobs, lone-parent households, renters (as opposed to people who own their own homes), people claiming key benefits, people with low education attainment, and people with long-term illness [*see* tables 4, 5, 6, and 7]. The factors cited above negatively affect poor people's future earnings, employment, and life situations far more deeply than they do people of greater means. Hence, it is not hard to see which people in the two LAs would be most deeply and negatively affected by cuts to public spending.

Another argument to explain the differences in the impact of austerity measures on our two example LAs is that wealthier populations have a broader council tax base, meaning that these LAs are less dependent on government grants and are more able to absorb grants cuts of the magnitude currently enforced by the central government (S&P 2009). In terms of our example LCs, K&C has a far bigger and broader council tax than Hackney. Therefore, this may be significant for explaining the difference in the impact on the residents of the two boroughs. Then again, the indices of spatial variation are important to consider in terms of explaining the difference in the extent to which austerity measures impact people in the two LAs. Nevertheless, the precise implications of these changes have been somewhat obscured by a range of approaches taken by LAs as they seek to balance their budgets. It has been acknowledged that tough funding for LAs in 2010 created significant financial challenges to service provision, marking a major shift from incremental growth. These cuts appear to signal the emergence of a new relationship between families and LAs. New trends are emerging as the thresholds for access to services are being redrawn.

Last but not least, the difference in political affiliation of our two example LAs can be seen as a factor that explains why people in Hackney are more likely to be disproportionally affected by austerity measures than people in K&C. As previously mentioned, Hackney is run by the Labour Party, whereas K&C is governed by the Conservative Party. The considerable difference in the level and range of services provided by the two LAs is to the result of opposing ideological views. The Conservative Party believes in the economy, minimal government intervention in both the market and citizens' lives, and the superiority of the private sector over the public sector (Elcock 1994). Furthermore, they believe that LAs must secure the lowest level of local taxation. On the other hand, the Labour Party is committed (in theory, though to lesser extent in practice) to more nationalization and less privatization (Vic and Edgell 1984). For the Labour Party, provision of public services is an additional tool to support and help those less wealthy and otherwise less-privileged groups in the society (Elcock 1994); Labour further believes that such services should, in the main, be provided by public authorities. The

Labour Party is also more in favour of government intervention in local markets and issues affecting citizens lives. This explains the Labour Party's reluctance to reduce public expenditures and why Labour-controlled LAs tend to have a higher local taxation (Elcock 1994). Conversely, the monetarist Conservative Party adheres to the exact opposite set of priorities (Vic and Edgell 1984). For Conservatives, reduction of public expenditures is a positive virtue (Vic and Edgell 1984). The Labour Party tends to promote more collectivism, while the Conservative Party has a strong commitment to individualism in the form of privatization. This, more than anything else, distinguishes the policies of one party from the other.

It is interesting to note that the two parties tend to converge when seeking a viable solution that will attract national support. A well-documented case that supports this is the invasion of Iraq in 2005 (and the military presence in Afghanistan), in which both parties demonstrated willingness to sending British troops. Nevertheless, the parties tend to diverge while seeking electorally viable solutions to problems. For example, both parties agree that the deficit must be reduced, but they disagree as to the pace of the welfare reform. It is the view of the Conservative Party that LA tax should be restrained and, therefore, that it should be kept as low as possible (Elcock 1994). This in turns means that LCs should confine themselves to meeting statutory rights and to supporting voluntary groups while embracing few worthy causes. In other words, for Conservatives, it is the obligation of all citizens to be responsible for making their own provisions and support, instead of relying on the LA to provide them (Elcock 1994). The Labour Party, in contrast, believes that services must be provided to all citizens who need them; that, as previously mentioned, raising local taxation has been a massive issue for LAs in Britain, in the sense that they exist and operate in an environment ruled by a central government that imposes certain standards by means of which service can delivered in exchange for money. Not complying with a central-government mandate means withdrawal of funds and other forms of punishment. This implies that the variation in spending power between councils depends on not only the scale of the cutbacks to their individual formula grant from government, but also the relative ability to get the best from the revenues provided by council tax and other sources. This latter proportion varies considerably between LAs, with some drawing a larger local tax base and therefore being less vulnerable to fluctuations in central-government grants. The pattern of cuts to public-service spending most affected the LAs that voted against the Conservative Party (which included Hackney), as these LAs were in fact hit harder by government spending (Dorling 2011). This is not simply because these deprived LAs were more dependent on government grants in the first place, or because government grants work in such way as to recognize the tax-raising abilities of different councils and allocate a greater proportion of funds to those councils with lower tax bases and with greater population density. All these situations are true, but more to the point, it is because the decisions made are driven purely by ideological views intended to achieve political gains. Perhaps most problematic of all is the fact that any analysis of spending inevitably becomes highly charged and politicized. Politicians are well aware of the impact of spending and taxation on people's voting behaviour. As a result, UK Conservative government

As our comparative analysis of the Hackney and K&C LAs has shown, to a certain extent some of the attributes outlined above not only play a vital role in comparing how austerity measures impact local government, but also that they are indeed the key factor necessary to measure the extent to which cuts to public spending affect people, their local neighbourhoods, and the LAs responsible for the day-to-day running of local affairs.

Conclusion

To sum up, it cannot be disputed that debates surrounding the impact of austerity measures upon people and local government in the United Kingdom is one that is highly complex and difficult to assess in totality. Some arguments stem from the notion of a capitalist ideology whereby there is promotion of neo-liberal agenda to maintain London's status as the world's premier financial centre. In contrast, the opposition highlights that this objective is a product of the extensive process of globalization. Either way, it can be said that economic policies that place a greater emphasis on inflation and cuts to public spending than on creation of jobs have brought much confusion and problems to ordinary people and local government. Consequently, LAs have been left with no choice but to pursue policies that are to certain extent detrimental to disadvantaged people. They have been force to comply with central-government directives to reduce public spending irrespective of the economic status of the LA and its inhabitants. LAs are urged to compete in an environment where the old economic and political distributions of power remain unchanged. Affluent neighbourhoods get away with this not only because they are likely participating in and influencing political process, but also because they have the ability to articulate their views. Given this evidence, we have highlighted throughout this book that the most-deprived LAs being undermined not only by the economic elements of globalization but also by the patterns of job distribution that continue to play an essential role in making the system work in favour of the rich and their more-affluent neighbourhoods.

The overall problem is that the approaches put forward to explain the extent to which austerity measures affect people and localities in the UK come from opposite ends of the spectrum. There is little empirical evidence backing up the positive impact of welfare policies in developed nations as well as in developing countries. Therefore, all the arguments presented are in some way limited and inconclusive, and as such, must be considered cautiously. The extent to which austerity measures impact people – either negatively or positively – will always vary from place to place, region to region, depending on the size of population, economic stage of development, demographic composition, degree of resilience of the population, political affiliations with the incumbent government, and so on. Any and all of these may play a major part. Given that disadvantaged urban communities have a high proportion of lone-parent households, renters (rather than individuals who own their own homes), unemployed individuals, people with long-term illnesses, people claiming benefits, people in the BME group, people employed in the public-service sector, people relying on the state for provision of services, and people in low-paying jobs, it is not hard to see which people will be disproportionally affected by the reduction in public spending. (Our comparative analysis of the LAs of Hackney and K&C in chapter 6 illustrated this.)

From the wide array of literature and empirical evidence, there is no doubt that austerity measures, to a certain extent, are more likely to have a disproportionate impact on people and households with children and larger families in a less-affluent neighbourhood in London (i.e. Hackney) than in an affluent Royal borough (i.e. K&C). Tables 4, 5, 6, and 7 in chapter 6 show that slightly higher percentages of people were affected in Hackney than in K&C. This is because of the substantial differences between the two boroughs, in terms of the demographic composition of the households and the employment and occupations of the residents. The brief analysis provided from the data used reveals a number of the things about these two boroughs and also shows clear spatial patterns associated with the explanations given above.

However, these two LAs have responded to their respective income shortfalls in different ways. The shortfall's impact on people locally has been overlooked by the fact that UK economy is expanding rapidly. At this stage, it is possible to reach direct conclusions from any these findings. Regardless, the underlying fact is that the environment has shown itself to be conducive for economic growth or downturn. As we have seen, the economy goes in cycles, with periods of higher growth and periods of lower (or no) economic growth. So, when there is a period of higher economic activity, there is substantial growth, and when there is a period of lower economic activity, there is a stagnation or recession. That is to say, the economy plays a big part in the contexts in which changes or policies are made.

For example, growth and demand in the United States helped bring the Canadian economy out of recession in the 1990s. As of this writing, the UK economy has grown to pre-recession levels. Germany and France have the played the biggest role in pulling the eurozone economy out of recession, and the eurozone is Britain's biggest market, similar to the case above, in which US growth and demand proved to be positive economic turning point for Canada. Much of the UK's success in reducing her welfare bill will depend in part on the fate of the eurozone, which is still weak. The fact that most European countries are reducing their public debt at the same time makes it difficult for their economies to grow, because restraining public spending means that there is no one available to buy and sell services. People hold on to their purses.

Overall, what is missing from the academic literature debates about the impact of austerity measures on people in Britain is any serious discussion of migration (political asylum and refugees). The idea of having an austerity measures in place is vague, in the sense that it is underpinned in ideological assumptions rather than scientific notions. Quite simply, researchers have found no evidence or convincing proof that austerity works. So the backdrop of Britain's core tenets of social-security provision has been changed forever. The welfare-benefits system created to provide people with a safety net in case of adversity has been weakened. The retrenchment is driven by ideology, and, unfortunately for people in the UK, the coalition government decided to embark on the easiest route of austerity policies, which punish those at the bottom of an already unequal society social and generate a huge amount of suffering unnecessarily. There is well-documented evidence to indicate that austerity measures are not only having a detrimental effect on people and LAs but also affecting voting behaviour. The number of families using food banks has nearly trebled since austerity came into effect, while the number of employed people claiming out-of-work benefits has risen from thousands in 2010 to a million (as of this writing). There is also an increase in the number of people claiming housing benefits, with millions of households on a waiting list and facing high housing costs (rents and mortgages), particularly in London. The price of essentials – such as food, petrol, and energy – have soared in comparison to wage increases. As a result, a huge number of families have seen their incomes squeezed by high living costs. Again, it is not hard to see which households are bearing the brunt of the savage cuts. [*Please see* the preceding chapters in this book for details on the foregoing summary.]

Unsurprisingly, voters are turning their backs to the main political parties in the UK. The main political parties failed to hold a majority of the votes in the last local elections, a feat not seen in more than hundred years. Similarly, the same situation has occurred across Europe, with a rise of far-right political parties in European elections. Whilst models to study human phenomena may work on most occasions, they fail miserably when crises arise. Thus, we shouldn't just focus our studies or interpretations of current social affairs and phenomena solely inform a theoretical standpoint; rather, we must also look at patterns of recurrence in order to reach a conclusive decision. This book has looked at some of these patterns of repetition and come to the conclusion that austerity measures are indeed exacerbating the conditions of people in poor neighbourhoods in the

UK, particularly BME, young people, and women. As of this writing more cuts are scheduled and will come into effect in April 2015; this implies that people and LAs in the UK will face even more financial and economic challenges. That said and as seen throughout this book, this is an evolving and very politicized issue; however, the true and full extent to which austerity measures impact people and LG in the UK will certainly be felt more acutely in the years and decades to come.

References and Resources

Books

Alesina and Ardagna (2002)

Almond, G. et al., *Comparative politics today: a world view,* 8th edn. (New York and London: Pearson/Longman, 2004).

Ashford, D., *Comparing public policy: new concepts and methods* (City: Publisher, 1978).

Bach, S. and Stroleny, A., (2013) Social dialogue and public service in aftermath of economics crisis.

Bagilhole, B., *Understanding equal opportunities and diversity: the social differentials and intersections of inequality* (Bristol: Policy Press, 2009).

Baylis, J. and Smith, S., *Globalization of world politics,* 3rd edn. (City: Publisher, 2005).

Blyth, M., *Austerity: the history of a dangerous idea* (City: Publisher, 2012).

Booth, P., (2014) "Radically decentralising power to town halls may pay UK growth dividend" Cited on city am newspaper

Byrne, A., *Local government in Britain: everyone's guide to how it works,* 7th edn. (London: Penguin, 2000).

Byrne, D., *Social exclusion* (Buckingham: Open University Press, 1999).

Chandler, J., *Local government today,* 4th edn. (Manchester: Manchester University Press, 2009).

Clark, J. et al., *Welfare, work, and poverty: lessons from recent reforms in the USA and UK* (London: Institute for the Study of Civil Society, 2000).

Clevel, P. et al., (1980) Urban and regional planning in age of austerity.

Darlington, R., (2012) New statement; tackle the deficit is driven by ideology.

Dan, C., *Public/private partnership: a marriage of convenience or a permanent commitment?* (London: Institute for Public Policy Research, 1997).

Dearlove, J. and Saunders, P., *Introduction to Britain Politics,* 3rd edn. (Cambridge: Polity Press, 2000).

Dorling and Thomas, *Bankrupt Britain: an atlas of social change* (Bristol: Policy Press, 2011).

Elcock, H., *Local government: policy and management in local authorities,* 3rd edn. (London: Routledge, 1994).

Fenwick, J., *Managing local government* (London: Chapman & Hall, 1995).

Gamble, *Britain in decline: economic policy, political strategy, and the British state,*4th edn. (Basingstoke: Macmillan, 1994).

Giddens, A., *Sociology,* 5th edn. (Cambridge: Polity Press, 2005).

Haynes, J., *Comparative politics in a globalizing world* (Cambridge: Polity Press, 2005).

Haseler, S., *Meltdown UK: there is another way* (London: Forum Press, 2010).

Held, D. and Kaya, A., *Global inequality: patterns and explanations* (Cambridge: Polity Press, 2007).

Hills, J. and Stewart, K, *A more equal society?: new labour, poverty, inequality, and exclusion* (Bristol: Policy Press, 2007).

Leyland, P., *The constitution of the United Kingdom: a contextual analysis,* 2nd edn. (Oxford: Hart, 2012).

Lowe, R., *The welfare state in Britain since 1945,* 3rd edn. (Basingstoke: Palgrave Macmillan, 2005).

Mason, D., *Explaining ethnic differences: changing patterns of disadvantaged Britain* (Bristol: Policy Press, 2003).

NIESR research report (2014) edited in evening standard newspaper in May 9 by Watts, J

Pearce, N. and Paxton, W., *Social justice: building a fairer Britain* (London: Politicos for IPPR, 2005).

Platt, L., *Migration and social mobility: the life chances of Britain's minority ethnic communities* (Bristol: Policy Press for Joseph Rowntree foundation, 2005).

Platt, L., *Understanding inequalities: stratifications and difference* (Cambridge: Polity Press, 2011).

Presbistero, A. and Eberhardt, M., research report (2014) cited in Giles, C financial times newspaper

Richard, and Smith (2005)

Sawyer, M., *The UK economy,* 16th edn. (Oxford: Oxford University Press, 2005).

Sklair, L., *Globalization: capitalism and its alternatives,* 3rd edn. (Oxford and New York: Oxford University Press, 2002).

Smith, D., *North and south divide: Britain's economic social and political divide,* 2nd edn. (London: Penguin, 1994).

Stiglitz, J., *Making globalization work* (London: Penguin, 2007).

Syke, R. et al., *Globalization and European welfare states: challenges and changes* (Basingstoke: Palgrave, 2001).

Talon, A., *Urban regeneration in the UK* (London and New York: Routledge, 2010).

Taylor-Gooby et al., *Welfare reform in the United Kingdom* (City: Publisher, 2001).

Todd, Knoop, A (2010) Recessions and depressions; understanding business cycles, 2nd edn. (Santa Barbara, California: Praeger, 2010).

Walker, A. and Walker, C., *Britain divided: the growth of social exclusion in the 1980s and 1990s* (London: CPAG, 1997).

Westbury, B. and Robert, S., *Government austerity: the good, bad, and ugly* (City: Publisher, 2010).

White, S., *Equality* (Cambridge: Polity Press, 2007).

Wildasky, A., *The politics of the budgetary process,* 1st edn. (Boston: Little, Brown and Co., 1964).

Journals

Broadshaw, J., "Research policy and planning", *Journal_of Social Services Research Groups* 14(1) (1986).

Hetling, A. and McDermott, M., "Judging a book by its cover: did perceptions of the 1986 US welfare reforms affect public support for spending on poor?", *Journal of Social Policy* 37(3) (2008), 471–485.

Vic, D. and Edgell, S., "Public expenditure cuts in Britain and consumption sectoral cleavages", *International Journal of Urban and Regional Research* 8 (1984), 177–196.

Websites

Hackney Council

http:// www.hackney.gov.uk

http://www.hmso.gov.uk

http://www.independent.co.uk/news/uk/politics/time-for-plan-b-imf-tells-george-osborne-to-ease-pace-of-spending-cuts-8627109.html (24/01/20130

http://www.theguardian.com/business/2013/jan/24/osborne-dismisses-imf-caution-fiscal

http://www.theguardian.com/business/2010/jun/11/europe-deficit-crisis-austerity-budgets

The Department for Work and Pensions (DWP)

http:// www.dwp.gov.uk/ads/statistics

The Department for Communities and Local Government (DCLG)

www.gov.uk/government/department/
for-communities-andlocal-government

The Greater London Authority

www.gla.gov.uk

Miscellaneous

www.demgames.org

www.dfpni.gov.uk

www.economichelp.org/macroeconomics/economicgrowth/
cause_recession

www.esrc.ac.uk/news_and_events/pressreleases/2853/new report
on the impact of recession on people's job business and
dailylives.aspx

www.gov.uk/government/uploads/system/uploads/
attachmentdata-data/file/316772/LGFS24_Web_edition

www.hmce.gov.uk

www.jrf.org.uk

www.local.communities.gov.uk/finance/0910/simpguid.pdf

www.neighbourhood,statistics.gov.uk

www.nomis.co.uk/report/imp/la

www.oxfam.org.uk /publications/multiple-cuts-for the –poorest-
families-175-million-of-the-poorest-families-have-31586

www.tax.org.uk

www.trusselltrust.org/stats.

www.uktax.demon.co.uk

www.voa.gov.uk/corporate/donwloads/pdf/vo7858-
understanding-ct.pdf